T0090023

FOUR TRIALS

JOHN
EDWARDS

U.S. SENATOR, NORTH CAROLINA

with John Auchard

SIMON & SCHUSTER PAPERBACKS

NEW YORK   LONDON   TORONTO   SYDNEY

Simon & Schuster Paperbacks
Rockefeller Center
1230 Avenue of the Americas
New York, NY 10020

First Simon & Schuster paperback edition 2004

SIMON & SCHUSTER PAPERBACKS and colophon are registered trademarks of
Simon & Schuster, Inc.

For information regarding special discounts for bulk purchases,
please contact Simon & Schuster Special Sales at
1-800-456-6798 or business@simonandschuster.com.

Designed by Jan Pisciotta

Manufactured in the United States of America

3   5   7   9   10   8   6   4   2

The Library of Congress has cataloged the hardcover edition as follows:
Edwards, John, date.
Four trials / John Edwards with John Auchard.
p. cm.
1. Edwards, John, date. 2. Lawyers—North Carolina—Biography.
3. Legislators—North Carolina—Biography. 4. Trials—North Carolina.
I. Auchard, John. II. Title.

KF373.E285A3 2004
340'.092—dc22
[B]
2003063005

ISBN 978-0-7432-7204-9

This, as everything I do, is for my children,
Cate, Emma Claire, Jack, and Wade

Contents

ACKNOWLEDGMENTS

It is the usual practice to use the acknowledgments page to thank the people who helped make a book a reality. And I will do that. But my real debt is to those people who made these stories possible, to the many men and women and families I have had the privilege to represent over nearly two decades as a lawyer. Whether or not their names appear here, each of those people and all of those families are precious to me, and every one has played a part in this story.

As far as these four trials, I hope that in this book my debt to many people becomes clear. Some have died—my sweet grandmother Pauline Wade, Judge Franklin Dupree, E.G. Sawyer, Bailey Griffin, and Bill Thorp—and I cannot thank them personally, but their importance to the book and to my life is not diminished now that they are gone.

I owe great thanks to men and women I have worked with: Bob Warner, Wade Smith, Roger Smith, Liz Kuniholm, Burton Craige, Andy Penry, Mark Holt, Kim Church, Bill Bystrynski, Andi Curcio, Laurie Armstrong, Gail Campbell, Jennifer Medlin, Betty Tucker Merkle, and Lisa White. And to Robert Zaytoun, Peter Sarda, Billy Richardson, Joel Stevenson, Sena-

Acknowledgments

tor Robert Swain, John Mason, O.E. Starnes, Jim Blount, Robert Clay, Alene Mercer, Gary Parsons, and North Carolina Superior Court judges Walter Allen, Herbert Phillips, Craig Ellis, and Robert Farmer. And thanks and appreciation also to Chris and Ashea Griffin, Charles and Libby Tate, Rick Tate, Kim Klocke, Lewis Reynolds, Beatrice Johnson Ingle, Wanda Davenport, Johnni Anders, Betty Seaman, Neil Thagard, Paul McMahan, Steve Snipes, Dr. Anthony Sciara, Cyndy Canty, Phil Smith, Sue Buck, Steve Bruce, and Tim Bruce.

And I particularly thank the families central to these four cases—for the trust they showed me and for their unfailing openness.

My thanks to Jeff and Peggy Campbell and precious Jennifer Campbell.

My thanks to the indomitable Golda Howard, courageous Josh Howard, and sweet Touché Howard.

My thanks and love to my personal heroes, David and Sandy Lakey, and to beautiful Valerie Lakey.

The contributions of Alyse Tharpe, Babs Nichols, Matt Leonard, Matt Nowell, Tyler Highsmith, Will Henderson, Gwynn Winstead, Thomas Sayre, Gene Hafer, Jim Jenkins, Diane Payne, Hargrave McElroy, Dan McLamb, and Andrew and Cheri Young cannot be put into words, but each knows his or her importance in my family's life.

I need also to thank the people who helped do the work to make this book more than a collection of papers and memories. I thank Mel Berger and Norman Brokaw at William Morris Agency and David Rosenthal at Simon & Schuster for their confidence in me, and Ruth Fecych for her guidance. I thank Christina Reynolds, John Dervin, and Bill Brady for the work to make certain my recollections were accurate, and Elizabeth Nicholas and Adrian Talbott for making the wheels turn whenever they got stuck. I thank David Ginsberg and Miles Lackey for reading and rereading with me, and for their honesty and loyalty.

And I thank John Auchard, who knows a good sentence when he reads one, and, frankly, when he writes one too, which he has done, and done again. He is a generous, perceptive, and eloquent man who has lent me his time and his talents, and this is a far better book because John is my friend.

And to the two men who have been as close to me as friends could be, and whose stories are completely entwined with mine: my deepest thanks to Judge J. Rich Leonard and David Kirby.

I must thank my family both first and last. I hope that their importance to my life and to all I do is clear to anyone who reads this book. Thanks to my entire family and particularly those whose role in my journey is part of this book, especially to my parents, Bobbie and Wallace Edwards, to my brother, Blake, and my sister, Kathy, to Rita Addis, Harold Addis, and Tim Addis, and to Vince and Liz Anania. And to my precious children, Catharine Elizabeth Edwards, Emma Claire Edwards, John Atticus Edwards, and Lucius Wade Edwards. Finally, my thanks to my wife, Elizabeth. I have spent many years trying to live up to what she believed I could be, and I am the better for it. This book and this life would simply not have been possible without her.

All of these people have shared their lives with me—some for weeks or months, some for decades—and many have dug out records and recounted memories so this book might be-

ACKNOWLEDGMENTS

come a reality. My debt to them continues to grow, and this acknowledgment is only an inadequate recognition of my growing obligation and my deep appreciation.

John Edwards
Raleigh, North Carolina

FOUR TRIALS

PREFACE

Before I was elected to the United States Senate, I served as a lawyer for twenty years. During that time I worked on several hundred cases, some of them big, some small, but all important—if not always to the greater world, at least to the people who walked into my office to ask for whatever help I might give. And important to me.

At first it seemed strange that so few people who came into my office were angry. In some ways they were probably beyond anger, for their lives had been altered completely—completely and forever—and they just sought something that could bring it back and make it good again. Anger might come later, or it might have been there before, but I almost never saw it in my office—for now they only hoped that things would change. So many of them were strong in ways I could not at first imagine, even some of those who could barely talk—for it is a strange thing to speak about your great pain to a man who has just gotten up from behind a desk and smiled at you. Some were not so strong at first, and many were still learning how to hold it all in as they moved through their new lives, gave formidable care to a husband or child or father, and worried about the future every minute of the day. A young woman with two young girls had lost her husband when a J. B. Hunt truck had run over and crushed him. Thin, blond, and frightened, she sat there and cried while her father did all the talking. When she began to talk, you could feel her relief, and her sense that someone might finally be there for her. Months later when the plumbing at her house went bad, she called our office for advice—and we were happy to send a lawyer out there to help her.

I keep coming back to the image of Ray Phillips. A huge bear of a man, Ray was a woodcutter and carpenter who had built all kinds of useful structures so that his severely disabled son might have a better world in their four-room mill house back in Hickory. "He's gonna get better. He's gonna get better," he began as he told me about the boy, but already tears were flowing down his cheeks and he knew that his son would never get better. I kept looking at him and his wife, sitting beside him, and I kept thinking how young they were, how innocent, how soft.

When I had to decide which few cases I would include in this book, I hated leaving out any of them, for I remember every person I met. I hated leaving out even those times I lost, for those people stay with me too, and besides, I had learned a great deal from those cases. I had learned how my work had to keep getting better, how I needed to know more and understand more, how I needed to consider with more imagination how good people might look at life quite differently.

During my years as an attorney, I developed a respect for juries as microcosms of our great and varied American society—where someone of sophistication and privilege sometimes sits right up beside a man who has never left the county where he was born, and who wouldn't complain about that fact for the world. Like every person in our society, every person on a jury has supreme importance. Any lawyer who forgets that is lost. When I entered public life, I felt lucky that I had already learned that lesson, and I don't forget it now.

It was in the courtroom that I learned how when you build a case, or anything important, every detail matters and every bit counts. And I learned that you can never for a moment forget the big picture or the broad ambitions of justice. I am grateful for those years, for it was then that I came to genuinely understand how smart and decent all kinds of regular American people are and will surely continue to be—even at the worst moments in their lives. I also learned how our great system can often discount the hardships and genuine suffering of such people—and how it can sometimes seem to forget their struggle almost completely.

In this book I offer only four cases, and it is a humble offering. But for many reasons these cases meant a lot to me—as did so many others. To be a member of the United States Senate is a great privilege, but in some ways it is no greater a privilege than to have worked with individual Americans, face-to-face and one by one, in the most intense situations of need and plain humanity, for twenty fine years. I hope that in telling a handful of their stories, this book tells the larger story of stubborn potential for the best kinds of change, and for more sure justice, in our quite remarkable American society.

E.G.

"I TRUST YOU."

E.G. Sawyer didn't speak these words. Instead, he typed them out on a plastic spelling board that had become his only means of communication since the day his life had changed six years before. It was a December evening in 1984, and my client and I sat on the ninth floor of the Buncombe County courthouse in an otherwise empty courtroom that overlooked the art deco cityscape of downtown Asheville, North Carolina. Only an hour before, I had completed my closing argument in an intense two-week trial where we had sought to prove that E.G. had been permanently disabled as a result of the medical malpractice of an Asheville doctor and the local hospital.

The next morning, the jury would begin deliberations. But for the moment as I sat beside my client, I wondered if I had done everything possible to make those twelve men and women understand the damage E.G. had suffered. Could they see the man he had once been—the real E.G. lost somewhere in the hunched and colorless figure that now slouched in a wheelchair? Back then this man hadn't needed a chair to get around or a spelling board to speak. This man had once been the freest of movers, the easiest of talkers; the kind of guy whose good looks and easy smile would always shield him—or so it seemed—from misfortune.

• • •

Howard E.G. Sawyer—those middle initials were an Appalachian quirk and stood for nothing—had long been accustomed to the power of his striking black-Irish good looks. He had known his charm pretty well, and he loved to talk and knew people loved to talk to him. He was a natural salesman, and a good one. When he drove his Chevrolet pickup around western North Carolina selling chemicals, slapping backs, and handing out gifts, he did more than distribute the usual fifths of Crown Royal or Jack Daniel's. He stocked up on baseball cards, penknives, and the like—for clients' kids and even for friends of their kid's.

E.G. Sawyer lived for the human exchange, and he loved the freedom his job gave him. No office, no time card—just a monthly quota he easily met but seldom exceeded. As soon as E.G.'s professional obligations were fulfilled, he hit the golf course. When he expanded his sales territory to the golfer's paradise of Florida, his boss, Charles Tate, could hardly complain. E.G.'s sales charm knew no state boundaries, and besides, E.G. took Tate's son along as his caddy.

The Tates had more or less adopted E.G., who lived in a neatly kept double-wide trailer just north of the Asheville city limits. He was a frequent dinner guest and a reliable presence during holidays. The Tates affectionately referred to him as "our bachelor."

Of course the ladies liked him too, for why shouldn't they—

even if he was a hard man to hold down, with all that moving and all that charm—and all that golf—which may have been his greatest passion of all. His first wife, Betty, continued to be fond of him even after she had left him, although she had long accepted that his real loves would always be the road and the links. And although he faithfully picked up their young children, Chad and Kim, each Saturday morning for swimming or baseball games, he loved his role as the Tates' bachelor at least as much as he enjoyed his role as Saturday dad.

But as E.G. entered his forties, as his sales chums and golfing partners abandoned him each evening for the tediums and glories of married life, bachelorhood lost its luster. In 1976, E.G. married again, a woman who was young, beautiful, and spirited—too spirited, it turned out, for the life E.G. envisioned. The marriage did not last a year.

His friends had never known him to drink—at all. While the others passed a whiskey bottle, an Orange Crush always sufficed for E.G., but when loneliness was accompanied by bitterness and humiliation, the once carefree man began a descent. In the privacy of his trailer, he began to drink whole fifths of vodka. For a full year, he kept his new addiction to himself, embarrassed by this latest failing. Then his sales performance began to slip. One day Charles Tate found E.G. in his trailer surrounded by empty bottles. He checked his employee and friend into St. Joseph's Hospital on Saturday, September 9, 1978.

•   •   •

I had just told E.G. that the defense attorneys had approached me with a settlement offer that he would need to accept—

or refuse—before the jury returned for deliberations the next morning. It was an offer of $750,000. E.G.'s fingers immediately stumbled onto the rickety plastic slab that sat just above his lap. That spelling board was supposed to prompt a synthesized voice for each word typed, but it constantly malfunctioned, so to understand what he was trying to say I generally had to watch E.G.'s once powerful fingers fumble against the letters. It was agonizing for him, and wrenching for anyone who watched him.

"Take it," he wrote, and although nothing had changed on his deadened face, I could feel his excitement.

For a moment I didn't respond. "Take it," his fingers wrote again—as if I hadn't understood.

I could hardly blame him. It was a lot of money—not just to my client, but to me, for E.G.'s working-class world was the world I knew. E.G.'s father drove a bus in Weaverville, just north of Asheville; my own dad had spent much of his life in the textile mills of North and South Carolina, where I was raised. In Raleigh, my wife Elizabeth still wore the $11 wedding ring I had bought for her seven years before. So when he said "Take it," I understood. I understood completely.

I had already talked with my partners and they were impressed with the offer and at first they seemed happy with it, but we all soon realized that in the long run it wouldn't be nearly enough to give E.G. any kind of life. The figure may have represented the sum of his lost potential wages, but that hardly meant anything for someone who could no longer walk or talk or drive, or cook for himself or dress himself, or even keep himself clean, or buy anything in a store or turn the pages of a newspaper or make any kind of plan for a different tomorrow. The settlement would merely house and clothe him, but E.G.—who deeply loved the freedom of his life on the road—could no longer function at all on his own. And the offer didn't come close to approaching the mountain of expenses for the medical and physical challenges that lay ahead as he grew older, feebler, and surely, more and more alone. They were hardships that we, and even E.G. himself, could hardly begin to imagine.

I had seen photographs of a tall, broad-shouldered man with big, muscular arms and a ready grin for the camera, but now he was the kind of embarrassing figure who one might turn away from on the street, eager to forget that kind of misery. He bore almost no resemblance to the winning fellow who once could have talked his way onto a golf course or into a woman's arms. It wasn't just that he was now fifty-one years old. It was that the armor he had worn into the world—the handsome face, the deft instinct for slapping a friend on the back or bending down and slipping a pocketknife to someone's shy son—had been stripped away. His black hair was now thinning and streaked with gray. His wide shoulders sagged inside the sports jacket I had wrestled him into that morning. His chin was damp; and his once lively eyes were vacant. And yet, he had this: the ability to make you believe in him and want to fight for him because, without any reservation, he believed in you in a way you did not yet believe in yourself.

He typed it out a third time: "Take it."

I told him it was not what he deserved, and it was not what he needed. "And let me tell you something," I added. "The jury knows it too."

E.G. sat there, his otherwise expressionless eyes welling up under the fluorescent lights. Then in a slow and halting manner, he began to move his hands.

"I trust you."

I trust you. I'll never forget how I felt at that moment, for E.G. Sawyer's message was the single most terrifying thing anyone had ever communicated to me. With those three words, he was putting his entire life in my hands. Trust me? I was thirty-one years old. Good grief, what did I really know?

I was telling this ruined man to turn his back on what must have seemed to him, what *was* to him, a fortune. And I was claiming to know what was in the jury's head. If I was wrong, E.G. would suffer even more miserably for the rest of his life—and I'd go home to my house and wife and children in Raleigh. And then on to my next case. I was all he had, and God help him, he trusted me. I felt scared.

But I had grown up knowing the world of E.G. and the strength of people in that world. They worked, and took hits, and they rarely complained. In bad times, sometimes the best they could think to do was turn inward—as E.G. did when he went back to his room—and sometimes that was in fact all they could do. My world is different now, and of course people close to me still suffer in real ways, but now many of them are powerful, and they have the privilege of knowing what to do and how to do it when son, daughter, mother, father, friend finds the whole world coming down. They pick up the phone and make a call, and it is often the right call. And then other calls are made that night, while they sleep or at least try to sleep. And sometimes—perhaps often—it does much good. Yes, this is my world now—I know that—and I can't deny that in many ways I am happy that it is. But all my life I have known people like E.G. or people like neighbors of E.G. I haven't forgotten what they are up against—in part because when I was young, I really saw what they were up against. And it is impossible to forget. When E.G. said he trusted me, I was genuinely afraid, but I knew that what we were trying to do was right. I genuinely believed that what we were trying to do could make a suffering man's life into some kind of better life.

My father, Wallace Edwards, worked for Milliken, the textile company, and since he was frequently reassigned to different mill towns throughout the South, we moved often when I was growing up. We'd pack up what we could from a mill house, and what we could not afford to move we'd leave to the church or to the next tenant. We'd drive off in our packed Ford sedan, and though she thought we didn't notice, my mother Bobbie would always turn to catch a last look at the house. We left half a lifetime's memories in sandy-lotted homes across the South.

I was surprised to find that mama had held on to an essay I'd written when I was eleven: "Why I Want To Be A Lawyer." Rereading it today, I'm struck first by the revelation that at one time in my life, my handwriting was actually somewhat legible. Once I get past the essay's half-decent script—like many in my office and home, I often can't come close to reading my penmanship today—I soon arrive at what I am sure was my key sentence: "Probably the most important reason I want to be a defense attorney is that I would like to protect innocent people from blind justice the best I can." Of course at that tender age I had no command of legal terminology. To an eleven-year-old, the concept of justice being "blind" sounded ominous, not one bit virtuous. Be that as it may, from early boyhood, what drew me to the law was the chance to "protect innocent people," to "give advice"—and even, I wrote rather grandiosely, to "save lives."

There were no lawyers in my extended family. There were millworkers, grocery clerks, ministers, Marines, boxers—but not lawyers. And though I barely knew Doc Smith, who was the only attorney in town, television brought all kinds of dramatic justice, and injustice too, into my small world.

As a boy I was moved, and I was shaken, by *The Fugitive,* that series where the wrongfully accused Dr. Richard Kimble escapes prison and roams the land in search of his wife's true killer. The show's depiction of "an innocent victim of blind justice" made a powerful impression on me, as it did on my whole family, and I remember my building fury when—week after week—no one ever bothered to take Dr. Kimble's side and make things right for him, or even try. Instead there was that constant grim detective whose only job, bankrolled by some remarkably lush federal budget, I later realized, was to find this one, single man.

And I was at least as fanatical about *Perry Mason,* but there I found real comfort in the show's last four and a half minutes when—week after week—that truly fine lawyer yanked yet another explosive confession from yet another cold, evil, and wily villain.

An optimist by nature, I always waited, in needless suspense, of course, for that final moment when wrongs would be righted, and righted in a flash. Now I don't even remember what happened in the last episode of *The Fugitive,* and although I suspect things turned out well for Dr. Richard Kimble, in my mind's eye he is still roaming the land and still searching for justice.

Of course it would be a few years before I made any connection between the people I grew up with and the glamorous victims I saw on *Perry Mason*—people whose hardship and suffering never lasted, of course, more than the sixty minutes allotted to each episode, minus the commercials. As an eleven-year-old I had no sense of how a man injured in a factory, or even just a regular salesman like E.G., might have the scales tipped against him as much as Dr. Kimble or the parade of clients lucky enough to have the services of Raymond Burr. In such cases those scales might remain tipped for life—especially if there was no one from their ranks who would stand up for them and provide them with a voice.

My dreams of righting wrongs yielded to dreams of buying a car. Then I found myself, as a high school student, working beside grown men building mobile homes. I thought I was earning the down payment on a red Duster, but I was in fact doing something else I did not realize until years later. I was imprinting the lives of those men on my sense of who I was and where I came from. I did the same at the mill when I swept the floors around the looms or when I painted markings on rural highways while I listened to a fellow named Brady tell me the woes of his life. By the time I left my parents' home to go to college, I had taken with me more than funny stories about the different colors Brady had dyed his hair ("Orange? You dyed your hair orange, Brady?" or "Dyed your hair black now, Brady?" "Naw, it's shoe polish"); I had also taken a sense of the dignity of hard work and the struggle of good men and women.

In 1977, ten years after the last episode of *The Fugitive*, I passed the state bar exam and on that same weekend married my law school sweetheart, Elizabeth Anania. We loaded up our small car and drove to Virginia Beach (where Elizabeth was to serve a one-year clerkship with Judge J. Calvitt Clarke, Jr.). And then I returned to Raleigh to begin my own one-year clerkship with U.S. District Judge Franklin T. Dupree, Jr. I regarded it as a small miracle that I'd gotten that far. It had taken hard work and, on the part of my parents, plenty of sacrifice. But I also had to believe it had taken some special grace to get me from the backyards of Robbins to a paneled federal courtroom in Raleigh.

A native of tiny Angier, North Carolina, Judge Dupree had already built a reputation as an excellent defense lawyer when President Nixon appointed him to the federal bench in 1970. He was the epitome of the old-school Southern establishment lawyer. He called his elegant and white-gloved wife "Miss Rosie" and pretended not to dote on her, though even to me, it was clear that he was both completely devoted to her and sure that he had married above himself. Many of his law clerks, particularly on his gruff days, agreed. He was at turns coldhearted and grandfatherly. And one of his joys was his annual birthday party, supposedly a gift from his former law clerks, who—now as lawyers who often practiced before him—knew to attend and pay their share of the Judge's and Miss Rosie's dinner. It was a command performance but few people minded.

Obtaining my clerkship with Judge Dupree was difficult not only because competition for the positions was always fierce, but also because of an additional hurdle: the Judge instructed me to show up for my job interview with my tennis racquet. It turned out that the sixty-four-year-old jurist was an avid tennis player who sometimes needed a partner when he was trying cases away from Raleigh. So we concluded the interview with a brisk set. I don't remember who won, but since I hadn't gotten the job yet, I'm going to guess that the Judge was the better player that day.

As I sat in Judge Dupree's courtroom, I came to understand how a presiding judge's philosophical leanings—the Judge was himself an ardent conservative—could shape the outcome of a trial in countless ways. A judge's influence is subtle but powerful. The parties and particularly the jury look to the judge as a rigorous protector of the law and take everything the judge says as serious, important, and impartial, whether it is the last of these or not.

In my year of watching trials at Judge Dupree's side, I also came to recognize those lawyers who did an exceptionally fine job and those who were less competent. I learned that knowledge is indeed power, but, most important, I learned that trials are about credibility—that if a jury is to believe in your case, the jury must believe you. You have to earn their trust, and after you have earned it, you have to earn it again, every day.

The twelve souls who spend full days, full weeks, or sometimes long months sitting only a few feet from you get to know you almost as well as you know yourself. They rarely miss a trick, and probably never when it really is a trick. They take in every movement, fact, word, hesitation, and glance. My faith in the wisdom of ordinary people took root in the mill towns of my youth. But the juries of my adulthood deepened that faith.

Juries seek the truth, and even as a clerk I learned that neither silver-tongued cunning nor hapless bungling will find it for them. They do not want to be manipulated, and they deeply distrust anything that makes them feel bullied—or hypnotized—into rendering a verdict. So the best lawyer must be honest and in a way plain in answering any doubts or confusions, and you must know the facts—all of them—for otherwise the jury will lose faith in you. As it should.

•　•　•

In September 1978, the same month in which E.G. Sawyer's boss drove him to St. Joseph's Hospital, I entered the law offices of Dearborn & Ewing in Nashville, Tennessee—my first job as a licensed attorney. Less than a month into that job, I began to learn some basic lessons I would need to learn if I was to be E.G.'s voice, and those lessons were not always easy.

The firm had just become engaged in litigation concerning a train derailment in Waverly, Tennessee. The derailed train was loaded with explosives, but it had lain seemingly harmless for days until, without warning, it exploded into flames. Nearly one hundred unlucky bystanders were killed or injured. The finger-pointing among the potentially responsible parties started right away, and one of the fingers was pointed at the manufacturer of the train's brake shoes. The manufacturer hired a firm out of Chicago to lead the company's defense and hired Dearborn & Ewing to help with the local depositions and with the byways of local Tennessee legal procedure.

The Chicago lawyer had been conducting a lengthy deposition of a key witness. When the other lawyers in the case started questioning the witness, the Chicago lawyer, who had to be in court elsewhere, called Dearborn & Ewing to get a local attorney to sit in on the remainder of the deposition. Although I knew little about the case, and even less about this witness, I was the only lawyer Dearborn & Ewing could spare at the moment, so off I went to my first solo deposition, and unwittingly to my first important lesson as a lawyer. In a deposition, a witness—who could be a party to the lawsuit, or someone who knows the facts, or an expert of some kind—takes an oath to tell the truth and then answers questions by the lawyers in the case. Depositions can last an hour or days. The Chicago lawyer's questioning of this witness had already taken a couple of days.

Because the case was so complicated and because there were so many plaintiffs and so many defendants, the deposition was held in a hotel ballroom, with white-linen-covered banquet tables. It seemed as if at least forty attorneys were working on the deposition, and they all appeared competent, confident, and unfazed by the surroundings. I was to listen to the other lawyers' questioning and to report what the witness said in case—well, I didn't really understand what I was supposed to do, so I just tried to listen and look as if I belonged. Fearing that I looked instead like a new and inexperienced lawyer, which I certainly was, I took a seat, scribbled down the brief conclusion of the deponent's testimony, and ducked out. I may have given my name to the court reporter, but other than that I did not say a word. When the Chicago attorney later asked me what the witness had said in his testimony, I gave what I thought was a reasonably accurate summary.

What I didn't know at the time was that the deponent's testimony that last day differed from what he'd said when the Chicago lawyer had asked him questions. I had not learned this from studying the transcripts or from reviewing the file or from listening closely to every turn in the witness's testimony. I learned this, unfortunately, from the Chicago lawyer, who ripped into me: "He testified to something different when I was questioning him than he did when you were there! And you didn't think to tell me that? What the hell were you doing in there? You're nothing more than a warm body!"

By the time he had finished with me, I was certain I had picked the wrong profession. But the man was right: in a deposition, as in trial testimony, a lawyer's got to listen to every word. A lawyer's got to be prepared, because a lawyer is the client's only eyes and ears, and voice. It was not easy to take that flaying, but I learned a lesson that made me a better lawyer in every other case I tried.

• • •

Nashville was good to us during our three years there. We bought a Southern colonial home with a lawn that spread under magnificent old oaks—and it all seemed like a palace to me. There in 1979, Elizabeth gave birth to our first child, Wade, and there we spent many late afternoons under those oaks watching him walk and run and grow. We would spend Saturday mornings roaming the Nashville flea market and Saturday nights at the antique auction in nearby Lebanon looking for furniture that we could refinish for our new home. And we made wonderful, lifelong friends.

Not long after we moved in, my parents took the ten-hour drive from Robbins to get a glimpse of our new life. I made a point of taking them to the City Club restaurant that topped the First American Bank Building and hovered over the glitter of downtown, the Cumberland River, and beyond. To be able to splurge like that for my folks, both of whom had worked long hours to put me through college, was tremendously gratifying. As we sat there and they remarked about how they'd never been up so high and never seen so far, I knew they were pleased with my life. I had no trouble imagining my dad at church the next weekend telling anyone who'd listen about the fancy place Johnny had taken them to in Nashville.

Still and all, the city never quite felt like home to Elizabeth and me. In the spring of 1981, we sent out resumes to various law firms in North Carolina, and by Memorial Day weekend, we were back in Raleigh.

It occurs to me, looking back now, that returning to Raleigh and taking that new job changed the course of my life—and not in small part because the job I took brought me to E.G.'s side. Tharrington, Smith & Hargrove in Raleigh was a small but dynamic law firm with a personality defined by two brothers, Wade and Roger Smith. The firm mostly handled criminal, family, and education law but was looking to expand its reach into civil litigation—a division that Wade Smith promised I could spearhead. I would be working on behalf of people, not big companies. The work sounded perfect—and I confess that I was taken by the Smith brothers. Who wouldn't be? Both had been captains of the football team at UNC and now both were outstanding trial lawyers. Roger was a poet, Wade played the banjo, and they understood how to practice law because they understood how to live a good life.

During my first three years there, the plaintiffs' cases that came our way weren't exactly monumental or even newsworthy. One involved a widow whose husband's will had bequeathed to her a life estate in his house along with a small sum of money. I saw the widow as a leaner Aunt Bea, who reminded me of my own grandmother, and I immediately liked her. And in fact, before the trial I discovered that she *was* a grandmother, the grandmother of our son's day-care teacher—and Wade saw the same sweetness in the young "Miz Dav'port" that I saw in her grandmother.

But the widow's stepdaughters, one of whom was executrix of the will, did not see it at all. They refused to honor the will and evicted her from her home. Not only did my client make me feel somewhat like Perry Mason, her stepdaughters played the roles of villains particularly well. We won the case. Fifteen years later, when I became a candidate in the 1998 U.S. Senate race, one of the sisters indicated her fond memories of me by proclaiming, "I would vote for O. J. Simpson before I would vote for John Edwards."

Other legal grievances came my way: a libel case for a small businessman who had been mocked by a competitor whose ads had turned my client's face into a monkey's face, a lawsuit over defective cable television boxes, even a case in which my client, a trucking company, successfully sued an insurance carrier that had denied coverage for an accident caused by a company trucker. It was good work, but I pined for a case that could swallow me up. I was restless when, in the summer of 1984, Wade Smith strolled into my office and plopped a thick file on my desk.

In his whiskey-smooth Carolina drawl, Wade said, "Senator Swain sent us this case from Asheville. He's about to settle it, but he wanted someone to look at it first."

I opened the file. Inside, I met E.G., and though I did not know it that day, I had found my calling.

• • •

The first time I saw E.G. Sawyer, on August 23, 1984, he was sitting in his wheelchair in a seedy one-room apartment on the east side of Asheville. The E.G. I had read about in the file, the sociable, good-looking charmer, was not one bit in evidence, and even the beaten E.G. who had turned his nights over to a bottle was not in the room. Slightly hunchbacked, with swollen legs and an unshaven face, E.G. Sawyer appeared to have been left there to rot. The room was his life: no family photos, no adornments of any kind, only creeping filth. The floor was blanketed with fast-food wrappers and cigarette ashes. A number of blue plastic cartons brimming with E.G.'s bodily fluids sat off in a corner, and the room smelled of urine. His fingernails were long and yellow. He wore a towel around his neck that he used to wipe off the saliva that constantly collected at his mouth, but because the saliva moved faster than his hands did, the front of his shirt was soaked. Mercifully, there was no mirror in sight.

E.G. had several good friends who brought him his hamburgers, paid his bills, and trimmed his hair—though the bleak spectacle of him was hard on them, and they'd begun to visit less and less. Each week a social worker dropped by to administer a sponge bath, empty the collection of urine containers, and pick up the garbage. E.G. could do almost nothing for himself—and was only the barest echo of the intrepid salesman who had always taken pains to keep his trailer neat and dress nice for the ladies. I shook his twisted hand, and he fought to say a few words, which did not quite make it out of his throat.

I don't remember exactly what I said to my client that first day. But I know what I was thinking. It's what I thought for the rest of that day, and in the weeks and months to come: *I'm going to get E.G. Sawyer out of this hellhole.*

• • •

How he arrived there was a tale that began with an act of kindness. On September 9, 1978, his boss, Charles Tate, insisted on driving E.G. to St. Joseph's Hospital. Neither Tate nor any of E.G.'s friends knew that E.G. had already visited the hospital six times that year for various ailments relating to alcohol abuse—after his second wife had left him, E.G. had slowly succumbed to his demons. In those earlier outpatient visits, his doctor, a skilled general practitioner in his forties, recognized the severity of his patient's condition. E.G. was wasting away.

Five days after Charles Tate checked E.G. into St. Joseph's, the doctor recommended aversion therapy—which would mean that E.G. would be given disulfiram, a drug better known by its brand name, Antabuse. If E.G. drank any alcohol, the Antabuse would make him nauseated and perhaps even profoundly ill, and ultimately, it would keep E.G. from drinking and allow the eventual repair of his liver function. E.G. acknowledged that the approach sounded like a good idea, and his boss and several other friends pledged that they would be there to keep up his spirits. So, on September 14, 1978, the doctor initiated the aversion therapy by prescribing the maximum daily dosage, 500 milligrams of Antabuse.

The next day, the fifteenth, the doctor prescribed double the maximum daily dosage of Antabuse for E.G., and on the sixteenth he tripled the dosage to 1500 milligrams. The doctor had attended a seminar in Atlanta in which this kind of aggressive therapy was discussed. The hospital's pharmacists dutifully filled the prescriptions, and the nurses dutifully administered them to E.G. Each day for the next two weeks he received three times the maximum daily dosage. Although at first he seemed cheerful and resolute about defeating his alcoholism, soon there were alarming signs that something had gone wrong. He complained of headaches and became increasingly drowsy and confused, and his blood pressure went up. On the evening of October 1, a nurse found him unconscious and lying crosswise on his bed. When Libby Tate, Charles Tate's wife, phoned the hospital the next day to see how the salesman was coming along, she was informed that E.G. Sawyer had been transferred to the intensive care unit. He was in a coma.

In December, E.G. emerged from his coma with extensive brain damage, unable to walk or talk without great difficulty. His friends transferred him to Duke University Hospital for continued treatment and therapy, then took him back to a rehabilitation center in Asheville. By that time, his transformation from robust and attractive man to a severely handicapped shadow of his former self was complete. On E.G.'s behalf, Charles Tate consulted four or five local attorneys, but none of them would take the case. Medical malpractice lawsuits had rarely been filed in conservative Buncombe County, and when they were filed, the results were usually the same: verdicts for doctors. Furthermore, no local jury was going to side against the beloved local hospital in favor of an alcoholic. When E.G. Sawyer was wheeled into the law office of state senator Robert Swain in the summer of 1981, the three-year statute of limitations—the period in which a lawsuit for negligence could be filed—had almost run out.

The veteran attorney couldn't believe it when he heard the name. Surely this was not the same E.G. Sawyer he used to see on the golf course. Swain's young associate, Joel Stevenson, listed the various reasons why the case was a sure loser. But Swain said, "If we don't help him, nobody will."

Still, Swain and Stevenson had never tried a malpractice case. After filing the complaint against the hospital and the doctor, they had little idea how to begin. So basically they did not begin. They took a few depositions, and then the case languished for the better part of another three years. As luck would have it, Senator Swain had recently helped kill a bill on the regulation of broadcast radio towers, and one day Wade Smith, who was also a lobbyist for the North Carolina Association for Broadcasters, stopped by the legislator's office in Raleigh to thank him for his effort. "If there's anything I can do to help you, just let me know," said Wade.

The senator replied, "As a matter of fact . . ."

A few days later, Wade Smith plopped E.G. Sawyer's file down on my desk.

• • •

The judge looked at me like I was crazy. Then he told me I was crazy.

"One and one-half million dollars? That's ridiculous. Why, you're just trying to get a notch in your belt, aren't you?"

The judge, the opposing counsel, Senator Swain's associate Joel Stevenson, and I were all seated in the law library of the Buncombe County courthouse. By all appearances the pretrial conference was going to be short. When asked by the judge what I thought it would take to settle E.G.'s case, I gave an honest reply. Considering that the overdose of Antabuse had rendered my client incapable of working, transporting himself, communicating effectively, or otherwise enjoying a normal life, compensation for the economic and emotional losses he had suffered should be at least $1.5 million. I hadn't pulled the number out of a hat: we had consulted with specialists about both E.G.'s projected lost wages and his ongoing medical and therapeutic needs. This was about fairness and justice, I told the judge, not about getting some notch in my belt. In fact, the idea of getting a notch in my belt with a medical malpractice case in the North Carolina mountains was on its face ridiculous. Of course I didn't say that. But even so the judge wasn't having any of it.

"Mister Edwards," he said. The words rolled out, as slow as molasses. "You may be able to get that kind of money back in Raleigh. But juries down here don't award more than a hundred thousand dollars. In fact, Mister Edwards..." He paused. "You introduce alcohol into a case in Buncombe County, and you lose. Now, whatever these gentlemen are offering here"—another pause—"you'd best take it."

"Your Honor," I said, "I think what I've proposed is the minimum of what's fair for my client."

Indicating the opposing counsel, the judge replied coldly, "Then if that's the settlement offer you have in mind, these gentlemen needn't even respond."

I left the courthouse *scared to death*. From close observation as Judge Dupree's clerk, I understood the enormous discretion a judge wielded during trial. How could I best represent E.G. when this judge was obviously hostile to me? He could effectively and subtly undermine E.G.'s case. In targeting me, the judge could hang E.G. Sawyer out to dry. My only hope was that when the trial was scheduled, this particular judge was nowhere near the Buncombe County courthouse.

I have mentioned that Senator Swain and Joel Stevenson had never handled a medical malpractice case before. Neither had I. Nor for that matter had any attorney at our Raleigh firm. Part of the reason for this inexperience was that such cases required a firm grasp of esoteric medical procedures and terminology, but the other reason was that, back in 1984, juries in a conservative region could scarcely fathom ruling against any doctor or any hospital in a civil proceeding. A car manufacturer, a restaurant, or even a police force might be held responsible for damages if its negligence had caused injury to someone. But the notion that a doctor could be liable for causing a patient lasting harm was difficult to square with the public's view of a physician as a benevolent and all-knowing lifesaver.

Of course, I could appreciate this sentiment. Doctors had delivered my children and had performed open-heart surgery on my father. All my life, I'd benefited from the fine work that physicians do. But physicians err like the rest of us, and when, through neglect or reckless behavior, they cause damage, they must be held accountable for the consequences of their action or inaction. The E.G. Sawyer tragedy was, to my mind, a classic case in point, for as a direct result of the doctor's administration of an outrageously high level of medication, E.G.'s life, although imperfect like all lives, had been ruined. The evidence couldn't have been clearer. My challenge would be to shatter the jurors' prejudice in favor of a good but mistaken doctor and against an alcoholic E.G. and to allow them see the facts for what they were.

First, I had to understand the facts. My client suffered from two disorders, encephalopathy and peripheral neuropathy—terms I didn't know how to pronounce, much less explain to a jury. (The first is a brain disease; the second involves damage to the nerves connecting the brain to other parts of the body.) I had to learn the nature of alcohol abuse and the pharmacological properties of Antabuse. I also had to develop an understanding of hospital protocol and how it had been flouted in E.G.'s case. In order to charge that the doctor and the hospital had violated the standards of care, I had to know just what the standards were. Through the discovery process, in which the defendants are compelled to furnish information relating to the plaintiff's case (and the plaintiff is compelled to reveal his evidence to the defense), I now had hundreds of pages of medical records to review. It was a detailed diary of E.G.'s deterioration, if I could only comprehend it.

• • •

I had to learn an entirely new language. But just as every mountain has toeholds, every language—legal, medical, political—has an accessible logic. The thing to do is to start. And when I started, I had the benefit of terrific help from two of Tharrington Smith's associates, Liz Kuniholm, who helped put the case together, and Andy Penry, who found an outstanding—and vital—expert witness willing to testify. Dr. John A. Ewing had recently retired as director of the Center for Alcohol Studies at the University of North Carolina at Chapel Hill. The sixty-one-year-old native Scotsman studied E.G.'s medical record and read the deposition testimony of the Atlanta "addictionologist" who had instructed the Asheville doctor that Antabuse could be administered in above-maximum dosages.

Dr. Ewing laid out for us, and subsequently destroyed, the doctor's likely defense. He felt confident that the doctor would argue that E.G.'s condition was caused by his drinking either before he was hospitalized or during the aversion therapy in the hospital. Since the hospital records showed E.G.'s consistent improvement, including improvement in his liver function, Dr. Ewing concluded the coma couldn't have been brought on by his prior alcohol abuse. Nor did he see signs that, as the defense had claimed, E.G. might have consumed alcohol during his hospitalization or that this alleged drinking had caused a violent reaction to Antabuse. This point had been especially worrisome to us since E.G.'s doctor had noted in his discharge summary that E.G.'s sudden deterioration suggested "the possibility of a drug inaction [*sic*] between disulfiram [Antabuse] and alcohol. The patient denied the surreptitious taking of alcohol. . . . Subsequently, it was learned by this examiner from the Intensive Care nursing staff that the patient admitted to surreptitiously obtaining alcohol during the time he was being treated with Antabuse." If this notation by the doctor was true, then of course E.G.'s case was sunk.

But Dr. Ewing seriously doubted this was so, and he used the medical records to prove his point. He told us that when an Antabuse patient takes alcohol, his blood pressure plunges. But according to the records, E.G.'s blood pressure had done the opposite and gone up—a sign of an overdose of Antabuse.

Still, the other side was undoubtedly going to cast our client as a hopeless drunk who had brought his miserable condition on himself. E.G. had denied to us that he had snuck a drink during his stay in the hospital, and the friends who visited him were just as adamant that they had not smuggled in any liquor. Although the doctor had ordered a blood alcohol test during E.G.'s decline, the result was never recorded, nor was there any record of the search, ordered by the doctor, for alcohol in E.G.'s room. But the doctor remained insistent that he had been told of E.G.'s drinking during hospitalization.

Two years before we were brought into the case, the doctor had submitted to a brief deposition in which he named his source of information for E.G.'s surreptitious drinking: a "red-headed" intensive care nurse named Miss Bonner. She was, unfortunately, no longer working at the hospital, and no one seemed to know where she was. The defendants were happy to have a swearing contest between a local doctor and an alcoholic.

• • •

Asheville, a wonderful town lodged in the hip of the Pisgah National Forest, is magnificent in the autumn, but I confess I don't remember the fall foliage in 1984. With Joel Stevenson's help, we located dozens of witnesses, among them old friends of E.G.'s who could help us paint a picture of what the salesman had been like before his hospitalization. We found experts who supported Dr. Ewing's opinion that the doctor's excessive administration of Antabuse had caused E.G.'s condition, hospital staff nurses and pharmacists who would testify that hospital personnel did not question the doctor's orders, and other experts who would reduce our client's needs and losses to monetary terms. And finally there was Dr. Margaret Burns, a psychiatrist who had treated E.G. in the early days of his hospitalization before the aversion therapy was initiated. She was the doctor who, when she discovered what the Antabuse treatment was doing to E.G., had ordered that it be halted.

After essentially gathering dust for nearly three years, the Sawyer case file was suddenly bulging. The defense attorneys were taken aback, for they'd been certain that Senator Swain would be an easy mark for a low settlement offer. Now they began to stall. We had forwarded interrogatories to the doctor's lawyers—written questions about the facts of the case to which the doctor was to provide written and sworn answers—but the doctor ignored the deadline for answering. Then the lawyers objected to our deposition scheduling and said they couldn't believe we had lined up so many medical experts to testify against another doctor. The list we submitted included experts they themselves had interviewed long before Senator Swain had brought Tharrington Smith into the case. When those experts told the defense that, no, they couldn't possibly side with the doctor, the attorneys committed the tactical blunder of not retaining them as "advisers." Instead they'd cut them loose, and now they were *our* witnesses. Since we were from out of town, to the defense lawyers we were an unknown quantity, but the fact was we were pretty much an unknown quantity even to ourselves.

In truth, I simply didn't know enough to be cowed. The more cases you try—and lose—the better sense you have of what can go wrong. No jury in Buncombe County had ever returned a verdict anywhere approaching the size we sought. Perhaps a more seasoned attorney would have agreed with the judge who told me I should settle for whatever the other side was offering. We may not have understood what all the risks were, and we may have been slim on experience, but we were young believers, and I felt we were just what E.G. needed.

Every chance I got, I visited E.G. Sawyer—partly to keep his spirits up, but at least as much to keep focused on what this case was truly about—and this happens in the legislative process as well—for it's easy to get caught up in the abstract fight. But these battles are never really abstract. Real people win and real people lose. Real lives change . . . or don't. So I would sit with a despondent fifty-one-year-old client whose world no longer knew golf courses, racetracks, or any open road. And we talked about his case.

Communicating in short bursts through his spelling board, wagging an index finger after the completion of each word, E.G. wanted to know everything. Was his old high school basketball coach willing to testify? He was. Had we located the redheaded Nurse Bonner? Not yet. Did I think E.G.'s doctor would take the stand in his own defense? Probably, and if not, I'd bring him on as an adverse witness. And where was that ice cream?

E.G.'s one remaining physical pleasure was chocolate ice cream. We would bring it to him by the half gallon, and he would push aside the spelling board and set the tub on his lap. While we emptied out his ashtrays and dumped out his urine bottles, he had a few moments of indulgence, and for that moment, he was transported from the grim apartment. Catching the hints of something alive in his eyes, I too would forget the room for a moment, but only a moment, and then I was back. This man hoped for a way out of his personal hell, and he thought I knew the way. I prayed I could find it.

In the days right before trial, after long hours of studying depositions, scribbling notes, after brainstorming with co-counsel, after organizing exhibits with the closest thing I had to a paralegal, my secretary Betty Tucker, I would finally retire to my bed at the Inn on the Plaza across from the courthouse. Lying in the dark among the scattered depositions and medical charts, I'd stare at the ceiling and see the shell of E.G. Sawyer, a ghost of a man in a wheelchair. Two, three hours of sleep at most, and then he would call me back to work.

•   •   •

From the windows behind the jury box of the courtroom on the ninth floor of the Buncombe County courthouse, you can see the museum dedicated to legendary Asheville author Thomas Wolfe, and, off in the distance, the southernmost spine of the Appalachian Mountains. Between these two points, St. Joseph's Hospital juts out of the cityscape. The hospital had evolved from a small sanitarium established in 1900 by the Sisters of Mercy, but now massive and stuck there on the side of the mountain, it appeared ready to throw its shadow, physically and psychologically, on the twelve men and women who would decide E.G.'s fate.

When E.G.'s case was scheduled for trial, I was relieved that it had not been assigned to the judge who had ridiculed the case in the pretrial conference. But the alternative was not reassuring. Superior Court Judge C. Walter Allen had never presided over a medical malpractice case, and worse still, his wife was an outpatient nurse at St. Joseph's. But Judge Allen, a tightly built man who ran a tight courtroom, was reputed to be fair. A stickler for efficiency, he was a strong believer in not burdening the court with lengthy trials and so he tended to push for settlements whenever possible. Above all, the judge saw opening arguments as a colossal waste of time, and he would interrupt any transgressor with a curt "Finish up. Let's get to the evidence. Bring up your witness." But before opening arguments came jury selection.

Jury selection for E.G.'s case began on Monday morning, December 3, 1984. In my view, no stage of a trial is more important than this one. Juries are just regular people. They are shop clerks, factory workers, secretaries, and teachers. They are the people I had grown up with in Robbins and in other mill towns. And they each come to the courtroom with their own lifetime of victories and heartbreaks and their own accumulation of biases. The point of jury selection is not to find twelve men and women who will definitely decide in favor of your client, for in my experience, such jurors don't exist. The point is to find jurors who will listen fairly to your case and will be open to your client's story and to you as the teller of that story.

When I was a lawyer, I had a view about jury selection different from some of my colleagues'. Some lawyers use jury selection to make arguments to prospective jurors about the merits of the case before the evidence begins. A lawyer does in fact need to present to them a general sense of what the case is about, and a lawyer certainly needs to identify those facts that could become problems in the case. But I never thought it was a good idea to make a speech during jury selection; for me, the closer jury selection was to a conversation around a kitchen table, the more effective it was. When I was young, I used to hear the saying "You can't learn anything when your mouth is open." Well, the same thing is true in front of a jury. If I was the one talking, I was not learning anything about the potential jurors, and so I wanted to get them talking; and better yet, I wanted to get them talking among themselves. When the closing argument was completed and the judge read them the law, I would not have a chance to speak to them again, but then they would be talking to one another in the jury room. The more I had a sense of what happened when they talked among themselves, the better able I would be to decide who among them would be fair to my client and who would emerge as their leaders.

So in jury selection, I might ask a particular juror what he thought about a certain issue in the case: Do you believe that a doctor shouldn't have to be accountable for his mistakes? Would you find it hard to have any sympathy for an alcoholic? Does the fact that you have friends working at St. Joseph's Hospital prejudice you? If we prove that the damages to our client exceed a million dollars, would you be unwilling to award him such a high amount? Would you hold it against my client that I'm a Raleigh attorney? Then I might turn to the juror next to him and ask what she thought about what he had said. I wanted to see their honest reactions and interactions, not just whether a juror was with us. But it's hard to turn a formal courtroom into a place where an almost intimate conversation can take place. The jury needs to forget the judge and the clerks and the other lawyers. When they do, a lawyer can really learn what he needs to know and can begin to build something essential in every case—a real relationship with the jury.

And I wanted to handle jury selection in E.G.'s case. But I wasn't the only lawyer; Bob Swain had signed on first. On the eve of trial, he reminded me that he knew these people.

drinking in the hospital was to blame for his condition. Second, and more significantly, Antabuse could indeed be administered at these elevated dosages despite the literature.

To attack these arguments, we began with E.G.'s psychiatrist, Margaret Burns. She was a compelling witness. Dr. Burns directly contradicted the doctor's 1982 deposition when she now insisted that the doctor had never consulted her about the massive dosages of Antabuse he prescribed to E.G. She testified that when she did in fact find out, she was "appalled and horrified," and on her own she suspended the Antabuse treatment—too late, of course.

On Thursday, we unloaded our heavy artillery of experts. And the best was Dr. Ewing. His thirty years of experience with Antabuse easily withstood a full day of cross-examination by Ed Harrell and the other two defense attorneys, O. E. Starnes and John Mason. As experienced as they were, these lawyers were no match for the Edinburgh-reared pathologist who had founded one of the nation's leading research institutes on alcoholism—and whose shock of white hair and keen Scottish voice clearly enthralled the jurors. Dr. Ewing was followed on the witness stand by three other doctors, each of whom backed up his opinion that only an Antabuse overdose could have induced E.G.'s coma.

When we finished presenting our broad range of medical witnesses, the defense had their chance to pull out their big guns. But the only expert they managed to call was the Atlanta addictionologist whose seminar had persuaded E.G.'s doctor that Antabuse could be administered in extremely high dosages. He was not a strong witness and was no match for Dr. Burns, Dr. Ewing, and the full cadre of other experts we had called. Ours would have impressed anyone.

The weight of the evidence was having its effect, and Ed Harrell had ceased his attempts at intimidation. Now he took to following me into the men's room, standing at the sinks, and muttering anxiously to me, "Can you let me out on a covenant?"

Let him out on a what? "Oh, I don't know, Ed, we'll have to see," I would reply.

"C'mon, John," he persisted. "Let me out on a covenant."

"We'll see, Ed." I had no idea what Ed was talking about. Only later did I learn that Ed Harrell was asking me to release his client, St. Joseph's Hospital, on a covenant not to sue. When I did find out, I had to laugh to myself. I might have been ignorant but I wasn't stupid.

Still, I spent the weekend worrying. By at least one significant measure, the opposition was noticeably unconcerned: the hospital's local insurance agent never once set foot in the courtroom. In cases in which the insurance company feared a verdict, I had heard, the local agent watched the trial and reported the progress to the company. I had not seen him in the courtroom even once. Did he know something we didn't? I had not forgotten the pretrial judge's admonition: *Introduce alcohol into a case in Buncombe County, and you lose.* I knew full well that medical data alone would not determine the outcome. Twelve computers weren't sitting in those seats beside the window. Whether I liked it or not, and regardless of the rules of evidence, it came down to this: the jurors weren't going to decide a thing until they heard from the doctor and from E.G. Sawyer himself.

Early on I'd decided to keep E.G. out of the courtroom. Rather than seat him beside me and let the jury grow accustomed to his presence, accustomed to his appearance, they should see him as I first had, as strangers would see him throughout his life. Monday afternoon, the time had come. After introducing into evidence several enlarged photographs of the once handsome salesman, and then allowing one of his closest friends to evoke the E.G. Sawyer of six years past, the present-day E.G. Sawyer was wheeled into the courtroom.

The jury's horror was palpable. Despite the nice blazer we'd squeezed him into, despite his recently trimmed hair, despite any and all efforts, our client could not be dandified. When he put his palsied hand on the Bible to take the oath, the oxygen seemed to be sucked out of the courtroom.

Senator Swain rose to his feet. "State your name," he said to E.G. Sawyer.

The senator let our client fight out those first syllables before asking, "Would it be easier to use your letter board?"

E.G. nodded, yes, it would be easier. Thereafter the senator gently guided him through his testimony. Even for those of us who knew the story, the poignancy of his testimony, literally spelled out for the jury, was hard to sit through. In his own gravel-throated manner, Bob Swain masterfully conducted a man-to-man and yet intimate dialogue with his old golfing buddy. And for once, when the senator concluded with his familiar "Examine him!" the challenge sounded appropriate.

Still, I was not prepared for what we were about to receive. Ed Harrell, bless his feisty heart, could not resist browbeating the witness in the wheelchair. First he hammered away at E.G. for the sin of not paying his taxes on time during the period of his hospitalization. Then, after reminding E.G. that the two of them had once played golf together, Harrell boomed, "And isn't it true that you cheated on your golf score?"

E.G. Sawyer: cheating quadriplegic. The jury was as

shocked as we were. By the time I wound up my legal career fourteen years later, I could still say that I had never seen a more disastrous cross-examination in all my life. And upon its conclusion, Judge Allen excused the jurors for the evening. They no doubt took with them the image of a poor crippled man being hollered at about some long-forgotten golf game.

• • •

I had thought much about E.G.'s doctor, and I had studied his career and pored over his writings and records. But since his deposition had been taken well before Wade Smith had agreed to help out Senator Swain with the case, I had never actually seen him until the trial. He sat at the defense table, a lean and prematurely white-haired gentleman who each day sported a different immaculately tailored suit. He projected an air of patrician indifference, as if these proceedings were somehow beneath him. When such a defendant takes the stand, as he finally did on Thursday, December 13, the worst thing an attorney can do is attack him, lest the jury be moved to sympathize with someone who has, by his own cold demeanor, already made himself unsympathetic. Instead, you simply take what the witness gives you, and he will often reward your patience.

The doctor took the stand late that morning. Examining him first was the hospital's attorney, O. E. Starnes, a veteran lawyer and member of the Asheville establishment: a street near downtown bore his family's name. The tale Starnes elicited was an altogether different one from that which we'd presented. The doctor had been treating E.G. Sawyer for one ailment or another since May 1976. As far back as then, said the doctor, the patient was a heavy smoker and a social drinker and was already experiencing an ominous tingling in his extremities. For well over an hour, the doctor enumerated E.G.'s visits, portraying him as either a hypochondriac or a self-destructive lout—or perhaps both. By 1978, as stated by the doctor, E.G. Sawyer was an alcoholic and a wholly unco-operative patient. By summertime, testified the doctor, "I was feeling my own despair. We had now six months of heavy and repeated evidence of the destruction of this man by alcohol, and I was not able to influence the course in any way."

When E.G.'s condition had stabilized after his admittance to St. Joseph's in September 1978, the doctor had recom-mended aversion therapy. E.G. would be given Antabuse, and it would cause him to avoid alcohol. But the doctor concluded that the usual dosage would be unlikely to produce a sufficient reaction, and since E.G. might still want to drink, he would probably discontinue the therapy. And so his only recourse, he testified, was a more aggressive dosage of Antabuse, about which he had learned at an Atlanta seminar. The doctor tes-tified that, alas, E.G. Sawyer had apparently sabotaged his own therapy. Midway through his treatment, he'd made omi-nous reference to a "blue pill" he'd been taking, presumably in addition to his prescribed medications—and that pill might have interfered with the aversion therapy. And as the doc-tor later learned from the redheaded Nurse Bonner, E.G. had been drinking in his hospital room as well. In the end, it was suggested, E.G. Sawyer's long history of abuse had caught up with him.

I began my cross-examination with that history. "Would it be fair to say that you want the jury to believe that on Septem-ber ninth, 1978, when Mr. Sawyer entered the hospital, that he was suffering from acute and chronic alcoholism?"

"Yes."

"But he walked into the hospital, didn't he, the best you know? He was walking while he was there, is that correct?"

"Yes, sir."

"He could talk while he was there, couldn't he, in September?"

"Yes."

"Could he walk when he left?"

"No."

"Could he talk?"

"Yes."

"He could?"

"If he closed the trachea, he could talk."

"Very, very limited fashion, though; is that correct?"

"That would be correct."

"So something happened. Can't we at least agree that something happened between September ninth, 1978, and December first, 1978, to Mr. Sawyer?"

"Yes."

"You were here when Mr. Sawyer came into the courtroom, were you not?"

"Yes."

"You're certainly not asking the jury to believe that the man you saw here on Monday of this week in the condition he was in, that he was in that condition on September ninth, 1978?"

"No."

Having refocused the jury's attention on E.G.'s period of hospitalization, I then moved to the doctor's understanding of Antabuse. I asked him to read aloud the maximum daily dosage for the drug from the *Physicians' Desk Reference,* the physician's and pharmacist's bible on the uses, dosages, and counterindications of prescription medications. Of course the maximum dosage was 500 milligrams, not 1500 milligrams. Then I asked him to review the literature put out by Antabuse's manufacturer, Ayhearst Laboratories. It recited the same maximum dosage. "You're not asking this jury to believe that as of September 1978 that you knew more about the proper dosage for Antabuse than the people who manufactured this drug, are you?" I asked.

The doctor waffled for a bit, but finally said no, he was not making that claim.

"Thank you, sir," I said. "What I'd like for you to do now, if you would, is to point out for me all of the written authority that existed as of September 1978 that would support a dose of Antabuse in the amount of fifteen hundred milligrams daily. Every one that you're aware of. I want you to tell me about all of them."

He could cite none.

I moved on to the doctor's assertion that E.G. had been drinking alcohol during his stay at the hospital. He acknowledged E.G.'s liver function tests had been improving during his stay, which was inconsistent with continued drinking. Furthermore, he conceded, "Alcohol was not detected," when the doctor ordered a blood alcohol test of his patient. And when he ordered the nurses to search E.G.'s room for liquor, "That was not found."

Finally, I referred the doctor to the discharge summary in which he wrote that "the patient's blood pressure was noted to rise, findings that suggest the possibility of a drug inaction [sic] between disulfiram and alcohol." Then I referred him to the entry for Antabuse in the *Physicians' Desk Reference*.

Would a drug interaction between disulfiram and alcohol cause hypertension, the rise in blood pressure that E.G. had experienced during his deterioration?

No.

What would such an interaction produce?

Hypotension—a drop, not an increase, in blood pressure.

In fact, the Atlanta "addictionologist"—the defense's one and only expert—had himself testified that he saw no evidence of an Antabuse-alcohol interaction in E.G. I felt that the jury had heard enough on this topic. Now I switched over to the doctor's secondary assertion—namely that E.G.'s current condition might have been caused by the patient's prior abuse of alcohol.

"Before this lawsuit was filed," I asked the doctor, "how many times did you ever indicate, either in your discharge summary or in any records you made throughout the course of your treatment of this man after September of 1978, how many times did you ever say that you suspected that his prior alcohol abuse may be the cause of his peripheral neuropathy and encephalopathy? How many times did you say that before this lawsuit was filed?"

"I never wrote it down," he admitted.

I handed the doctor an evaluation done by the neurologist to whom he had referred E.G. after E.G. had come out of the coma suffering from encephalopathy and peripheral neuropathy. "Does Dr. Martin ever identify Mr. Sawyer's alcohol abuse prior to September ninth, 1978, as a cause of his encephalopathy and peripheral neuropathy?"

"He does not say that."

I questioned the doctor on his earlier testimony that at the time of his admission E.G. was suffering from "acute and chronic alcoholism." I referred him to his admission summary, which actually described E.G. as having a less severe condition—"episodic alcoholism."

"In fact," I said, "the first time in any of your records that you say that this man was a 'chronic alcoholic' is when you do your discharge summary on December thirty-first, 1978, three months after he goes into a coma; is that correct?"

"What is correct," he countered, "is that I did not appreciate or know that Mr. Sawyer's alcoholism, whether it began in December of 1977 in a significant way or January of 1978 where it was becoming clear-cut, was of the magnitude, the persistence, and the degree to which I subsequently learned." He carried on for a minute more.

But I believed we had him. As with many of the juries I would face, few if any among E.G.'s jury had graduated from college, and sometimes a witness would try to overwhelm such a jury with technical language or overblown explanations. But the jurors all had good common sense, and I was sure they could tell that the doctor was not answering the question.

I turned to E.G.'s condition when he had been transferred from St. Joseph's to Duke University Hospital.

"Looking at the discharge summary," I said, "you have listed as number one, 'alcoholism, acute and chronic.' But his principal problem during the period of October through November 1978 was not alcoholism. It was encephalopathy and peripheral neuropathy, wasn't it? He almost died, didn't he?"

"Yes, and respiratory difficulties of major proportions."

"And you have listed in your final diagnosis as the second item, 'encephalopathy and peripheral neuropathy,' haven't you?"

"Yes."

"All right. Doctor, you were in the courtroom on Monday when Mr. Sawyer came in, weren't you?"

"Yes, sir."

"You saw the condition he's in?"

"Yes, sir."

"You don't want to feel like you're responsible for that man's condition, do you?"

Ed Harrell shouted out his objection. Judge Allen sustained it. A party's motives in his testimony are relevant, but I did not complain. My point was made.

With an Antabuse-alcohol interaction and E.G.'s prior alcoholism pretty much dispensed with, I finished with the doctor's far-fetched third possibility: that mysterious "blue pill" E.G. had requested. I asked the doctor what he made of it.

He replied, "The significance was that there was a medication or there was some pill which Mr. Sawyer knew or stated that he knew he was receiving, and I did not know what it was. He could not give me a name of it, and a search of everything that I knew that he was receiving didn't fit with that description."

I approached the doctor and handed him a list of the drugs he had prescribed for E.G. beginning with E.G.'s admission on September 9. One of them was Limbitrol. I handed him a photograph of the pill. What was its color?

"That is blue," he said, but added, "That drug was discontinued on, I believe, the second day"—meaning, the tenth of September. The doctor had testified that E.G. was asking for the pill after the aversion therapy was started on September 14.

I asked him to reread the order sheet. No, he now acknowledged, it was discontinued on September 16. And when, according to the progress notes, did E.G. say that he wanted the blue pill?

The doctor again referred to the progress notes. The seventeenth, he said.

$$\bullet \quad \bullet \quad \bullet$$

We had only one rebuttal witness, though she was enough: Kim Bonner.

An associate of Joel Stevenson's had located Nurse Bonner in Michigan. In the frenzy to bring her to Asheville in time for rebuttal, we had not thought to ask her what she knew about the lawsuit. And so we didn't know that the defense had in fact located Nurse Bonner months before. They had flown her down to Asheville, hoping to put her on as one of their witnesses. When they learned what she had to say, they promptly flew her back to Michigan and hoped that she would never turn up again. The expression on their faces when the tall, attractive, twenty-nine-year-old redhead strode down the ninth-floor hallway and into the courtroom was as stricken as her testimony was succinct.

I asked her: Had E.G. Sawyer told Nurse Bonner that he had consumed alcohol during his stay at St. Joseph's Hospital?

"No."

Had she told the doctor that E.G. Sawyer had said such a thing to her?

"No."

After Nurse Bonner's testimony, Judge Allen called both sides into his chambers. An otherwise fair and cool-headed man, he had reached his limit. "You guys had better do something about this," the judge said to the three defense attorneys. Pointing to me, he said, "He's made a liar out of your guy! Now, where the hell is your insurance carrier? If you don't come up with some kind of settlement, I'd say you're in deep trouble."

And the opposition finally did, just after our closing arguments. But I persuaded E.G. to let the jury decide. That was when he wrote "I trust you" on his letter board.

That night I prayed I was worthy of his trust.

•   •   •

Because you just can't know, finally. When the jury is in the courtroom, you can watch them. Although they generally try to sit sphinx-like, as if to convey their impartiality by their stillness, they are human beings. But you can tell when they are confused, and then you try to clarify. You can see when they just don't believe something, and you can elicit evidence to eliminate their doubts. Yet when the door to the jury room closes, you can no longer rescue your client's case from confusion or doubt. As I have said, the jury is a microcosm of democracy. If a candidate has not made a case persuasively enough, once the curtain on the voting booth is pulled, it is too late to make it. Believe me, when that jury door closes, you tear yourself apart: Did I make it sufficiently clear that an Antabuse-alcohol interaction could not have induced E.G.'s coma? Was I too hard on the doctor? Did they accept the numbers relating to damages?

From the other side, John Mason had delivered what I thought was a brilliant closing argument for the defense, one that methodically built a composite of E.G. Sawyer as a secretive alcoholic bent on self-annihilation. I'd followed his argument with an impassioned declaration that "their main defense, and main goal in this case, is to throw mud on E.G. Sawyer—which is *infuriating* to me." And it was. But had I gone overboard? For all our efforts, had we simply been unable to relieve the jury of prejudices against an alcoholic?

Those four hours of deliberations on Tuesday, December 18, felt longer to me than the preceding two weeks of testimony. I spent them in that little courtroom, consumed with self-doubt and staring out the window at the mountains and the hospital.

The four men and eight women returned to their seats late that afternoon. The verdict sheet was handed to Judge Allen. I saw his jaw go slack. Then, finding his voice, he instructed that the verdict be read.

Was Howard E.G. Sawyer injured by the negligence of the defendant, the doctor?

"Yes."

Was Howard E.G. Sawyer injured by the negligence of the defendant, St. Joseph's Hospital?

"Yes."

What amount, if any, is Howard E.G. Sawyer entitled to recover?

"Three million, seven hundred thousand dollars."

• • •

On the steps of the courthouse, Senator Swain was holding a press conference. I waved to him and headed for my car, for E.G. did not yet know the verdict, and I wanted to be the one to tell him.

Within three months, E.G. Sawyer would be out of his shabby apartment and settled in a small farmhouse right near his daughter's home in Tennessee. For the first time since that week when his life changed completely, E.G. had the care he needed, a sense of dignity back in his life, and some genuine excitement for what the next day might bring.

JENNIFER

⬤══➤

Late in the evening of July 17, 1979, Elizabeth went into labor, and I drove her to Baptist Hospital in Nashville. For nearly twenty-four hours she remained near delivery. Nurses and residents came and went from her room, reading monitors I did not understand and making notes in charts I could not read. I didn't ask questions, but I simply maintained a nervous vigil and stayed close, a helpless twenty-six-year-old husband. The wails of anguish that came from another room echoed through the entire wing as a mother gave birth to a stillborn baby. As Elizabeth was having contractions and nurses moved in and out of the room, and a fetal monitor spit out a steady stream of ticker tape, the wails went on and on. Even when they finally stopped, they were a bigger presence in our room than anything else. Yet our little drama continued to unfold.

When at one point the nurses wheeled Elizabeth to X-ray, I did not know enough to be concerned. A resident read the pelvic X ray and said everything was fine, but hours later when our obstetrician read the same X ray, he frowned and rushed Elizabeth to the delivery room. He recognized what the resident had not, that the baby would not be able to fit through the pelvis, and so he prepared for a cesarean delivery. Hospital policy being what it was in 1979, I was left at the delivery room door.

On the other side of that door, Elizabeth lay on a delivery table with a tent over her legs and abdomen. While the anesthesiologist hovered over her face, she strained to listen to her obstetrician and heard him say to an assisting physician, "It's dead." The stillborn baby fresh on her mind, she was frantic. "What did he say?" she asked the anesthesiologist, who simply leaned closer but did not answer. Elizabeth did not know that they were talking about the cauterizing machine, which had lost power. It was nearly midnight on July 18 before she was finally relieved by the sight of our son, alive, healthy, and loud.

When they brought him to me, fresh from delivery, the top of his head was covered with a blanket. I pulled it back, and my newborn son was—for the moment, at least—a conehead! From the effort to wedge through the pelvis, he was discolored and bruised and his head was tapered to an unmistakable point. He was also the most beautiful thing I'd ever seen. I took him to the newborn nursery and returned to Elizabeth in the recovery room. All I could think to say to her was "Thank you for giving me what I always wanted."

Along with the day nearly three years later when Cate was born, and the days several years later that brought the births of our children Emma Claire and Jack, that day will always rank among the memories I treasure most. The birth of one's child should always be like that, and it should never be the nightmare that it became for Peggy and Jeff Campbell.

• • •

The strongest people do not always appear strong. Jeffrey Lawrence Campbell and Margaret "Peggy" O'Shea Campbell were both open-faced, wide-eyed, and young on the late morning they entered Pitt County Memorial Hospital in Greenville, North Carolina. Jeff was a solidly built former high school wrestler whose father was a supervisor at the local Procter & Gamble plant, where they manufactured Pampers. On the day he first met Peggy at a youth group meeting at Temple Free Will Baptist Church, he had just turned seventeen. The fifteen-year-old brunette with a glowing smile was far too shy to let on to the young boy that she was attracted to him, but the group leader heard her giggling and whispering to the other girls, and he urged Peggy to grab the seat next to Jeff—which she did. Jeff turned to meet her piercing brown eyes, and that was that. As they drove to dinner on their first date, a drunk driver rear-ended the '65 Ford Fairlane station wagon Jeff had spent all day waxing. That evening the couple wound up filing accident reports at the police station, both afraid that Peggy's strict father would blame Jeff and end their courtship.

But Mr. O'Shea did no such thing, and in fact eighteen months later on February 4, 1978, during Peggy's last semester at Greenville Christian Academy, he proudly gave his daughter away when she married Jeff. Mr. O'Shea had a friend who got the newlyweds free tickets to Disney World, so Jeff and Peggy drove 640 miles to Orlando for a four-day honeymoon— the last real vacation they would take until their twenty-fifth anniversary. When they returned to Greenville, nineteen-year-old Jeff accepted a lithography job at his father-in-law's printing shop, but wanting a trade of his own, he soon started on at Winterville Machine Works as an apprentice machinist.

Happy to be more of his own man, Jeff began talking with his seventeen-year-old wife about a powerful ambition they both had, to raise a family. When six months later Peggy became pregnant, they had already picked out several names—all of them girls'.

In the early months of the pregnancy, the Southern heat took over their tiny rental home. Jeff worked nights, and Peggy felt anxious when she had to sleep alone. Although they had no air-conditioning, before she went to bed, she went around the small house and shut all the windows tight and locked them. Her husband would be gone until his eight-hour night shift ended at 5 A.M., and when he arrived home, the first thing he would do was open the windows and let the house breathe a little.

But at least that graveyard shift left Jeff with free afternoons, and so he was able to take Lamaze classes with Peggy—and he loved them. It was a revelation to them, especially to him, that—these days—a husband might actually participate in the birth of his child, and that he might actually learn enough to understand what every stage, every movement, and every baffling effort of his wife's labor really meant. It amazed him that he might come to know what his wife was really doing in her struggle, and what even the baby was trying to do—for the baby was struggling too—until that astonishing moment when he would first hold his child in his arms, and then, still amazed, hand the baby back to its mother.

Toward the end of Peggy's pregnancy, Jeff's performance at Winterville Machine Works won him first-shift status, and so he would be able to wake and sleep with his wife and child. Everything was progressing well, so when one day a doctor expressed a hint of worry, it seemed only that, a hint of worry.

Near the end of her term, when Peggy was examined by a young doctor at a Greenville OB-GYN clinic, he informed her that the fetus was in a breech presentation—meaning, positioned either buttocks-down or feet-down in the womb. He assured her that although this was no real cause for alarm, the fact had to be made clear to the hospital staff as soon as Peggy was admitted for delivery. It would be necessary for the staff to determine, as the critical first step, if the fetus was still in a breech position. If it was, the young doctor concluded with an apologetic smile, then a cesarean would be required. And a cesarean, he assured her, was nothing at all unusual.

Peggy told him she was scared, so he tried to prepare her for what to expect—she would go to an operating room, the doctors would make an incision in her abdomen, and she would stay in the hospital five days. But Peggy was still frightened. For a moment, she felt like a child herself and was overwhelmed by this complication, but then Jeff played his sturdy part, calmed her down, and reminded her of the most important thing, that their baby was healthy. He, however, was worried enough to ask the young doctor, when he saw him at a Lamaze class, whether the baby was still in a breech position. It was. Could the baby be turned? No, it could not; if the baby was in a breech position, a cesarean would be necessary. But the doctor reassured them that they were right on schedule for a late-April delivery, and yes, the baby was healthy.

As it turned out, Peggy's contractions began when expected, just after she awoke on the morning of April 30, 1979. She called Jeff at work—he had just arrived there—and he raced home to monitor his wife's contractions, just as he had been trained to do. At 11:30 A.M. the contractions were five minutes apart, and a minute later Jeff was helping Peggy into the same '65 Ford Fairlane in which they had gone on their first date, and then he drove quickly to the emergency room entrance of Pitt County Memorial Hospital.

It is a ritual so many of us know and one that Elizabeth and I would repeat three months after the Campbells: the entrusting of our dearest hopes to a battalion of strangers dressed in white. Such surrender is complete—a leap of faith that is warranted by countless feats of casual heroism at every hospital all across America. And so Jeff and Peggy began their experience at Pitt County Memorial without the slightest reason to believe that the outcome would be in any way different from ours. Peggy was asked to sit in the familiar wheelchair and was taken off to the labor and delivery admitting room while Jeff stayed behind in registration to answer the familiar questions about doctors and insurance companies. In the admitting room as Peggy was prepped for labor, she found things going just as her Lamaze teacher had described them, and she remembered to instruct the staff to check the fetus's presentation. After Doctor D., her obstetrician, examined her, she was wheeled to the X-ray room, while Jeff trotted alongside and blurted out words of clumsy reassurance to his wife. As they began to succumb to the comforting rhythms and the clean expertise of the Pitt County Memorial delivery staff, the Campbells relinquished their fate to the hospital.

The coming hours would find Peggy in terrible discomfort, and then, after she was given Demerol to relieve the pain, deeply medicated—but at all times helpless. And Jeff felt almost as helpless as he waited outside the door during the pelvic X ray and then in the labor room at his wife's bedside. The attending nurse was continually in motion: jotting notes on a labor flow sheet, checking Peggy's temperature and pulse, examining the progress of her dilation. The nurse said little except when, on the telephone outside Peggy's room, she discussed matters with the obstetrician. At 2:30 P.M., after one such phone conversation, she strapped an external fetal monitor around Peggy's abdomen, and little clicking noises started up as the monitor began tapping out what would become a long ticker-tape strip. By reading the lines on the monitor strip, the doctor and nurses could trace Peggy's contractions and the baby's heart rate, all of which would provide a window into the womb and indicate how the baby was dealing with the stress of being born. The nurse waited for a contraction and checked the strip; the fetus was responding well to the stress of labor, and all seemed fine.

Through the fog induced by the Demerol, Peggy overheard one of the nurses say something that at the time carried no particular significance—except that it was uttered in tones of surprise: "He's going to let her deliver."

Peggy did, however, know who "he" was. Peggy's obstetrician, Doctor D., worked at the Greenville medical center with the young doctor who had first told the Campbells their fetus was in a breech position. With a mollifying smile and a confident manner, Doctor D.—significantly older and more experienced than his young partner—had conducted a brief examination of Peggy in the admitting room, then popped his head in a few times while she was in the labor room. Though he seemed amiable enough, to the Campbells he projected an air of authority that brooked no disrespect and hardly even a question. When one of the nurses had been slow to administer the initial dose of Demerol, he had snapped at her, "When I give you an order, I expect you to do it."

So it was with some hesitation that Jeff intercepted Doctor

D. and asked if he would be C-sectioning Peggy. The obstetrician, however, did not hesitate. No, he replied, from what he had seen in the pelvic X rays, he was going to "let her go." Jeff took that to mean that everything was proceeding normally for a vaginal delivery. Jeff was under the impression—from the nurses or from Doctor D. himself—that the X rays had shown a baby in a breech position. But Doctor D. did not elaborate about "letting Peggy go," and Jeff was afraid to bother him— and he was sure the doctor would be bothered—with any more questions. Instead, he returned to Peggy's bedside and continued to coach her through her labor, just as he had been trained to do in the Lamaze classes. He squeezed her hand, kept her on top of her contractions, and assured her, "You're doing good," while the attending nurse watched the fetal monitor and made notes on her clipboard.

Jeff noticed that the nurse seemed concerned with the readings she was getting on the fetal monitor strip. At times the heartbeat tracing disappeared altogether, but that was a common problem with external monitors and moving babies during delivery, so the nurse shifted the apparatus from one side to the other until she found a location where she could catch the baby's heart rate. She assured Jeff that losing the heartbeat during a contraction was not uncommon. But on more than one occasion she called Doctor D. into the room and expressed concern that, although the monitor was reading the baby's heartbeats, the heart rate had slowed enough to worry her a bit. The doctor examined Peggy each time and each time declared that the heartbeat had rebounded and that Peggy's progress was normal.

At one point during a pelvic examination, Doctor D. commented, "I believe I feel a scrotum." The words did not seem to register with the nurse who stood beside him and never lifted her eyes from her clipboard. But it certainly registered with Peggy and Jeff, for they had only picked out girls' names. A boy? They looked at one another uneasily, naive to the real reason for alarm. Then Doctor D. left the room and returned, as they learned later, to another labor.

By 6:50 P.M. the baby's fetal heart rate had again slowed, and when it did not rebound, the nurse again called for Doctor D. He quickly determined that Peggy was fully dilated and ready for a vaginal delivery. Jeff's heart quickened, for after months of Lamaze training, he was eager to assist at the delivery of his child. But to his surprise and dismay, Doctor D. instructed him to stay behind. "Stay in the room, and I'll send for you when the baby is born," the obstetrician told him, congenially enough but without explanation or any other comment at all.

Peggy was unconscious and Jeff was not present when at 7:04 P.M. Doctor D. performed a total breech extraction. The baby's clavicle, which would have been forgiving in a headfirst vaginal delivery, was fractured during the breech extraction. The newborn had no scrotum and was in fact a girl, a ghostly pale girl, with the umbilical cord wrapped tightly around her legs. Her Apgar scores—an assessment taken immediately after birth that quantifies heart rate, respiration, reflex reaction, and other factors—registered at 1 out of a possible 10 at one minute after birth and then 2 out of 10 at five minutes, indicating the slimmest of life functions. Although the hospital did not have a pediatrician on duty, fortunately one was present in the hospital who could perform emergency neonatal resuscitation. He leaned over the baby, working her chest and forcing air into her lungs—for forty minutes. Finally the pale baby girl began to breathe on her own. It was nearly 8 P.M. When Peggy awoke from the anesthesia, Doctor D. told her, "She's fine. She just had a little trouble breathing." And then a tired but happy Peggy was taken to the recovery room.

At 8:40 P.M., the attending nurse returned to the labor room where Jeff was anxiously waiting. She told him that his baby was a girl and that both mother and child were doing fine. Those were the only words Jeff wanted and needed to hear, and so when she held out a form for Jeff to sign, consenting to the delivery of the baby, he simply saw it as the ratification of his and Peggy's dream. That Jeff Campbell was being asked to "consent" to an event that had already occurred, that he was being asked to sign such a document well after the baby's birth, did not trouble him at the time.

A few moments later, Doctor D. himself spoke to Jeff. Now a second person told the new father that his baby was fine. Although Doctor D. volunteered that the baby had experienced trouble breathing, this detail seemed offered as trivia, as almost ancient history. Jeff thanked the doctor. Gone were the unsettling questions concerning the talk of a scrotum, the anxiety in the labor room, and the frustration as the delivery room door had closed in front of him. He and Peggy had a little girl, and as soon as he was able to visit his wife, they agreed upon a name: Jennifer Love Campbell. When the nurses told Jeff that he could not stay over for the night, he told Peggy he loved her and headed home for a few hours of sleep.

Peggy shared a room with another new mother, who now held her baby in her arms. But when Peggy asked to see Jennifer, the nurses told her that she should rest up first. She later repeated the request, and again she was urged to get some sleep. After that, no nurses visited her room for the rest of the evening. She longed to see her baby, and so she was frustrated and unsettled. But it had been an epic day that had left her too weary to mull over the implications of any evasiveness on the part of the nurses, and so she did fall asleep, and she slept soundly.

Early the next morning when Jeff arrived at Pitt County Memorial, he was met by a doctor he did not know. It was the pediatrician who had performed emergency resuscitation on Jennifer the night before. "Your daughter's in intensive care," he told Jeff.

Jeff was stunned and he struggled to find words. Then the questions tumbled out, one after another. Was Jennifer all right? Remembering Doctor D.'s report, he asked if she was having trouble breathing, and the pediatrician's grim expression was sufficient answer. Another question and another, and finally the question Jeff would remember most: Did she have brain damage?

When the doctor would not say, Jeff bolted toward Peggy's room, only to find her standing at the nurses' station, in a state much like his own—afraid, confused, and feeling unbearably helpless. Peggy was haggard and angry as she asked again and again, Where was her baby? Why were they giving her the runaround?

"Peggy, sit down," Jeff said, for he knew that the little the pediatrician had just told him was more than anyone had told his wife—although she had been asking questions for over an hour. While he cradled Peggy, another pediatrician came over to them, then led them into a small office and closed the door behind them.

Perhaps he spoke with some sensitivity, yet the only words the Campbells heard were these: "Your daughter has gone into seizures. She'll probably be a vegetable. She may very well die. If she doesn't, do you want to keep her?"

It was for them the moment when their world completely changed. Hours before they had entertained visions of their daughter in the crib they had bought, of a happy baby, a cheerful toddler, a growing child, and of themselves as happy parents. And now, abruptly, that vision had been supplanted by one of tremendous fear, and already a kind of grief.

And yet the question was shocking. *Keep her?* This was their child. Even as the singular image of their wide and happy future crumbled, they had no doubts. Of course we will keep our daughter. There is no question.

• • •

The staff relented and led the Campbells into the intensive care unit, where for the first time they saw their baby. She was writhing with seizures and screaming without pause. Peggy began to cry at the heartbreaking sight of their child, a child who knew nothing of life but suffering, an intense suffering that never seemed to let up. Peggy and Jeff moved as close to Jennifer as they could and tried to see something in her face that gave even a hint of some joy to be alive. But they saw nothing like that.

They were told that there was nothing they could do, that Peggy would be discharged and Jennifer would stay at the hospital. So Jeff checked Peggy out of Pitt County Memorial Hospital and drove her home to what was a quiet and empty house.

Two days later, Doctor D. drove up to the Campbells' small rental home to conduct a routine checkup on Peggy. By now the couple had visited Jennifer several times and had seen for themselves that, although she remained in the ICU, her seizures had somewhat abated and she was not in fact "a vegetable." Still her status remained unclear, and Doctor D. was as stingy with details as he had been in the past. When he simply stated that Jennifer would be in the hospital for six to eight weeks, Jeff and Peggy chose to take no report of any additional bad news as proof that their daughter was improving. In fact, when nine days later a nurse at Pitt County Memorial called to say that Jennifer was ready to be picked up, their hopes began to rise. Jeff and Peggy brought their daughter home. Although they had been warned that Jennifer would have to be tube-fed, they found that she could with some difficulty drink from a bottle. She was better than they had been led to expect, and although the Campbells gave their thanks to God and assured each other that the worst was over, it was not.

Three months after leaving the hospital, Jennifer Love Campbell was diagnosed with cerebral palsy.

• • •

It was not in the Campbells' nature to cast blame. Like me, they were devout Christians, and their first impulse was to count Jennifer's survival as a blessing. She was a gorgeous child, with her mother's encompassing brown eyes and a radiant smile, but as she approached her third birthday, Jennifer remained unable to walk, her speech barely intelligible, and her cognitive abilities retarded. Although Jeff had landed a better-paying job and Peggy had given up plans to attend nursing school in favor of devoting all of her time to Jennifer, proper care for their daughter far exceeded the Campbells' modest means. Despite all of this, and in spite of prodding by family and friends, Peggy and Jeff were reluctant to complain about the medical attention Peggy had received when Jennifer was born. They refused to question Doctor D.'s decision to forgo the cesarean that the Lamaze instructor and even Doctor D.'s young partner had told them would be necessary. Not wishing to spend their energies on something that could not be remedied after the fact, they fixed their sights on their daughter's present and future, and they tried to keep up their spirits.

But there was no denying that over time certain questions began to plague the Campbells. What did it mean that Doctor D. had said he could feel a scrotum, when of course there had been no scrotum? And why had there been such a disparity between Doctor D.'s general nonchalance and the attending nurse's worry over the fetal monitor readings? Then why did the obstetrician refuse to let Jeff into the delivery room—something Jeff and Peggy had been assured would be possible, even welcomed? And why wasn't Jeff told the reason he was being kept out? And what was the motive behind the request for signatures on that delivery consent form—a request made, and made so emphatically, only after the fact? As the Campbells thought more clearly about what had happened at the hospital almost three years before, many things seemed to have happened in the shadows—or had been pushed into the shadows.

As Jennifer grew, as beautiful as she was in many ways, her parents saw how their innocent optimism had been just that—innocent, and perhaps somewhat foolish. Who could have blamed them for their early hopes? Their friends supported them in many ways, but everyone began to understand how bad things really were with Jennifer, and how bad they had really been from the start. One day, a friend intervened and prompted the Campbells to take the initial step. She handed Jeff the name of a lawyer she knew, Peter Sarda, a partner at Kirby, Wallace, Creech, Sarda & Zaytoun in Raleigh.

Although Peter and the other talented partners at Kirby Wallace were shaken by the story of Jennifer Campbell—as was everyone who came in contact with the remarkable little girl—the firm had no experience with such cases and they knew it. Here was a child who had been severely injured by negligence, by gross negligence on the part of a physician, as well as on the part of the hospital itself. Although the little girl's suffering was great and the injustice of her situation appalling, Kirby Wallace knew what it would mean to fight against that doctor and that powerful hospital. To do the job right, the young attorneys would need to marshal many forces and call in many experts, as they would take depositions, do complicated medical research in specialized areas, work up exhibits, and search for witnesses out of an already receding past. Up front it could cost perhaps $100,000, and if the case was lost in court, that staggering expense would easily strap a firm of only five lawyers. And to make matters more grim, the doctor and the hospital had already recruited Jim Blount and Bob Clay. They were the two finest defense lawyers in North Carolina.

But Kirby Wallace took the case. It was impossible not to take it for Jennifer. For two years, Peter Sarda and Robert Zaytoun worked hard on behalf of the Campbells, breaking new ground every day, but they were increasingly aware of how unfamiliar they still were with some of the tangled considerations in medical malpractice cases. As the opposition of

Jim Blount and Bob Clay came to seem more formidable than ever, David Kirby suggested to his partners that the case—and above all the Campbells—needed the expertise of a proven medical malpractice attorney, and that's when my name came up. David and I had been friends in law school, and he had followed the E.G. Sawyer case with great attention. So the decision was made to add a new counsel to the effort, and on Christmas Day, 1984, Robert Zaytoun dropped off the Campbell file on my back porch.

One morning in January 1985, I pulled into the driveway of the Campbells' little brick house in Winterville—a house they had just purchased with a government loan. Although the trees were taller in the town where I had grown up, and my family's house had been larger, their neighborhood reminded me of my own Robbins neighborhood, where the small front yards up and down my street looked pretty much the same. And at the sides of the houses I saw other things familiar to me: sometimes a car on cinder blocks, or sheets and pillowcases held on lines by wooden clothespins, a basketball backboard and hoop nailed to a pine tree, or stoops crowded with houseplants put out in the sun for the day. It was a neighborhood of children and their self-sufficient, hardworking parents.

Meeting Jennifer Campbell was nothing like my first encounter with E.G. Sawyer, for unlike E.G., she was far from alone. Beside her parents, Jennifer already had a little sister, Rebecca, and another baby was due any day. All around her there were the signs of things little girls love, and signs of a little girl who was loved. Her playpen—for even at nearly six, Jennifer needed a playpen—sat right in the middle of the living room and she was surrounded by a riot of toys. And there were lots of dolls—I'm not so good at the particulars of dolls, but I have since learned enough to suspect there were Barbies, maybe tons of Barbies, in there with her. At the corner of the playpen there was a tall feeder that allowed her to climb to her feet and stand up, so that she might align her spine while she ate. The feeder shocked me at first, amid all the brightly colored things.

The room was spare but inviting, for Peggy had a real knack for making a house into a home. There were good chairs and a good sofa, and the kind of assorted bric-a-brac that makes people think of their own parents' home. It sure made me think of mine. The Campbells had in fact made a fine home, and it seemed a happy place.

But I had read their file and I knew the reality they faced every day. Jeff and Peggy were cheerful and welcoming people, and in spite of how hard things had gone for them and for their daughter, you saw that anger was an uncomfortable emotion for them; they did not like to complain. They smiled a lot and tried to act as if everything were fine, even as they answered my questions and described, in necessary painful detail, what a day in the life of their daughter was really like. They had taken Jennifer out of the playpen, and I had greeted her and she had greeted me back with her startling smile.

As I spoke with her parents and she crawled around the room, I saw that her hands could never manage to lie flat against the floor, so she was forced to claw into the carpet as she moved about. Although she was getting big, she couldn't walk, and her knees were covered with calluses. There is something terrible about calluses on a child.

My own beautiful son Wade had been born only three months after Jennifer, but at the Salvation Army, I was already coaching him in basketball, and already Wade seemed to have big plans. He was a joyous child, who found something new each and every day, who had the capability to dote on his little sister Cate, and as I sat there and talked to the Campbells about their child, I never forgot the wonder of having Wade. I watched Jennifer smile, and I watched the Campbells smile, and I'm sure I smiled back. My heart broke for them.

By the time I met the Campbells in January, the trial had already been scheduled for late March. I had little time to prepare, but I knew from experience that delays of any kind can invite unforeseen obstacles, and so I decided not to ask for a continuance. Although I knew I would have to work round-the-clock to catch up and be absolutely prepared for the trial, I was ready for that. I was more than ready.

But the Campbell case would involve a whole lot more than speed or endurance. The Sawyer case had been a walk in the park by comparison. In Asheville, I'd found a somewhat complacent defense team, a wholly unsympathetic doctor defendant, and a balanced jury pool. None of these factors existed in *Jennifer Campbell v. Pitt County Memorial Hospital.*

There was a reason why, in 1985, young law firms like Kirby Wallace or even established law firms like Tharrington Smith, for which I worked, seldom took on a case like Jennifer Campbell's: you were sure to lose your shirt. Medical malpractice cases were expensive, and physicians and hospitals, much beloved by the public, were happy to take their chances with a jury, so fair settlements before trial were rare. In addition, the medical profession protected the sanctity—and range—of their "professional judgment" by generally refusing to testify that another doctor's treatment fell below the established standard of care. Blessed though we were to have top-notch experts testify in E.G. Sawyer's case, they were hard-won. In spite of the Asheville doctor's obvious error in prescribing E.G. three times the maximum dosage of Antabuse, two specialists we had contacted before trial had refused to say so in court. After all, health-care professionals who did not back one another often faced unpleasant repercussions. In 1981, Bill Thorp, a legendary North Carolina attorney, won a $1.75-million lawsuit on behalf of Larry Downs, a young man who was admitted to Duke Hospital for cleft palate surgery and, as a result of a grossly improper extubation, lapsed into a four-month coma and was eventually declared brain-dead. The frank testimony of the attending nurse made the verdict possible. She paid the price, however: shortly after the verdict, she was fired from Duke.

When Burton Craige, a lanky, energetic young associate at Tharrington Smith, became my associate on the case, it fell to him to round up doctors and nurses to testify as expert witnesses. By the end of January, he said he felt like a telemarketer, he had been hung up on so many times. A few doctors were candid in admitting that they'd already reviewed the Campbell file on behalf of Pitt County Memorial and that they had told the hospital that it looked like a bad case. Would they testify to that effect? Uh . . . sorry.

But on January 21, Burton reported to me that he'd been wildly successful. A retired department head from the OB-GYN department of the University of North Carolina Medical School had reviewed Jennifer's file and told Burton that "999 out of 1000 obstetricians would have performed a cesarean section under these circumstances." Believing himself to have an obligation to the public, the retired doctor declared that he would testify. Jennifer had her star expert.

A week later, the retired doctor called Burton again. He'd spoken to a few other physicians he would not name and he said he now wished to reconsider his opinion. Burton talked the retired doctor through the points he'd raised earlier. The man wiggled out from under every one of them. He said that he would return the $400 retainer fee.

Some of such reluctance stemmed from feelings for the defendant. Doctor D. was a pillar of the eastern North Carolina medical community—a man who had delivered some seven to eight thousand babies since beginning his medical internship in 1955. He was an obstetrician from the old school. Although the growing availability of antibiotics had made cesareans far less risky, Doctor D. remained committed to vaginal delivery. He just plain never thought about cesarean sections, didn't like them. Undoubtedly many of the OBs we contacted saw Doctor D.'s ways as outmoded. But it pained them to denounce a mentor figure—and undoubtedly, some of them feared the consequences of doing so.

In all, Burton contacted forty-one obstetricians. Of these, thirty-six either flatly refused to testify, would not return Burton's calls, or waffled so badly that they essentially disqualified themselves as witnesses. That left five who were willing to testify. Of these, two were from in state, and one rambled so badly that we knew we couldn't put him on the stand. So our arsenal of homegrown expert OBs numbered exactly one. Burton fared much better among nurses: twelve refused or ignored us, but four said yes. Of course, the defense could select from the statewide medical personnel directory to line up support for the biggest hospital system in eastern North Carolina.

That was an advantage the two lead defense attorneys hardly needed. Doctor D.'s counsel, James D. Blount, Jr., had been practicing law since 1952, the year before I was born. He had an immensely powerful presence and in the courtroom was a linebacker among water boys. Bespectacled and bulb-nosed, with a marvelous baritone voice, Jim Blount had an undeniable way with jurors, and with the opposition too: he could nice you into a state of paralysis. And although you would never know it to see this country lawyer cajole a witness and work his wide-bodied charm, Blount's firm, Smith, Anderson, Blount, Dorsett & Mitchell, was establishment Raleigh all the way, and deep in talent, experience, and resources.

You could get into a lively argument over who was the best defense lawyer in North Carolina, Jim Blount or Bob Clay. Stylistically, the two resided at opposite poles. Ten years Blount's junior—but still seventeen years ahead of me in legal experience—Clay was given to bright sports jackets, which formed the perfect pedestal for his truly impressive helmet of prematurely white hair. He used his glasses as a prop, moving them up and down his nose to indicate his disbelief, dry amusement, or pure disdain. While Blount had the voice of God, Clay really looked the part—or at least he looked like a pretty impressive TV evangelist. Furthermore, no one in the state bar had more experience trying medical malpractice cases, and he was not shy about letting you know it. He had begun as a plaintiff's lawyer and had at one time won the highest personal injury award in North Carolina on behalf of a man who had been lobotomized by a tire rim when the tire he was filling had exploded. Sick of losing to Bob Clay, the state's largest insurance company, St. Paul's, hired him as counsel in the early 1980s.

Bob and I are now good friends, and my respect for his talents has never faltered. Even back then he had a way about him and was so sure of himself—with good reason too—that he seemed to expect everyone else in the room to immediately know who he was. As the "old defense counsel for your local county hospital," Clay would get calls from doctors who over lunch downtown had heard the opposing counsel discuss strategies they were planning against him. I'm sure he took those calls as his due. Then he used what he had gotten without apology, always ready to deploy his full arsenal and intimidate people in court.

My feeling was that if Clay wanted to play the bully in front of the jury, I sure wasn't going to stand in his way. While we tried to be unfailingly polite to his witnesses—and it wasn't easy—he loved roughing up ours. He was particularly aggressive with the well-respected University of North Carolina economist Dr. J. Finley Lee, someone many lawyers regularly used to testify concerning lost-wage calculations. Clay insinuated that the taxpayers were subsidizing Lee, that his calculations were deviously padded, and that our expert was nothing more than a tweedy con artist.

I tried to short-circuit his tactic—and I did—by asking a question that turned those insinuations back on Clay himself. "Dr. Lee," I asked, "have you done any consulting work, economic consulting work, for members of Mr. Clay's law firm in the past? Or would you rather not answer that question?"

"I would prefer not to talk about that," answered Lee. "I think who I work for is proprietary." The point was made. I have talked about the importance of an attorney's credibility, and this is not a secret only I know. Bob Clay knew it well, and he knew he would lose credibility by attacking a witness as a fraud whom he had used on his side in other cases.

Clay and I had a history. When Elizabeth and I'd decided to

leave Nashville, I'd interviewed with his firm, Patterson, Dilthey & Clay, before deciding to go with Tharrington Smith. And after the E.G. Sawyer verdict, the insurer of St. Joseph's Hospital, St. Paul's, sent Clay to Asheville to do some cleanup work on the disbursement of funds. While expressing some admiration for our victory, Bob Clay let it be known that if he had been leading the defense team, the outcome would have been substantially different.

I'd been hearing that sort of thing ever since the Sawyer verdict began making the rounds. *Edwards snuck up on 'em. Edwards got lucky. Edwards won because of his hair.* I still thought E.G. won his case because he was right and because he had lawyers who believed in him and worked for him as hard as they knew how.

Jennifer's case was just as right as E.G.'s, but there was no denying that Jennifer would need everything we could bring to the case and, to win against Bob Clay, maybe a little luck. Whatever had happened in Asheville, it was safe to say that we wouldn't be sneaking up on any lawyers in Greenville.

• • •

The judge, Judge Herbert O. Phillips, was a laid-back jurist in his sixties who, despite his long years on the bench, had tried few if any cases remotely similar to *Jennifer Campbell v. Pitt County Memorial Hospital.* To his credit, he did not pretend otherwise, and he frequently solicited the lawyers' guidance on a legal matter. When Bob Clay supplied his spin on things, he inevitably began with "Having been in a number of these things before" or "I have been up this road a time or two in the past." On one occasion, Clay took a not-so-subtle swipe at me when he declared to the judge that "even the greenest lawyer" should know a particular point.

My fellow UNC alumnus Michael Jordan will tell you that basketball games aren't won by slam dunks or even great style. What happens in a game is more often determined by the pregame hours devoted to practicing, studying tapes, and getting to know what to expect from the opposition. Similarly, the outcomes of trials are not determined by courtroom theatrics but rather by the most intense preparation possible. Though the trial of *Campbell v. Pitt County Memorial Hospital* would be among the most dramatic in my legal career, the stage for its outcome was set, as is so often the case, during pretrial depositions.

It's hard to relish deposition-taking. At bottom, it's about eliciting all the information and opinions that a witness for the other side intends to disgorge—although sometimes it is more like squeezing every last bit of toothpaste from a tube, and oftentimes, about as exciting. In any case, even if what is gathered is important, it often does not seem so earth-shattering at the time, for until all the evidence is gleaned and brought together, it is impossible to know which pieces will be the key pieces of the larger puzzle.

Although at the outset we had seen the Campbell case mostly as one against Doctor D., we soon came to recognize serious negligence on the part of the nursing staff and on the part of the hospital in general. In particular, the attending nurse had stood by while the obstetrician had consistently ignored fetal monitor signs indicating that Jennifer was experiencing acute fetal distress. We believed the nurse had a duty to act, but we also knew that such an argument would be hard to sell to a jury. For generations, people believed that the attending physician was the "captain of the ship" and by analogy that any questioning of the doctor's wisdom was mutiny. But that analogy is dangerous and pernicious, for here the ship is the patient's life. The patient has a right to depend on the doctor, the nurse, and every health-care professional to treat his or her obligation to the patient as superior to any obligations to one another.

Traditions die hard, and our one local expert obstetrician, a fine gentleman from Durham County General Hospital, went down in flames during depositions on this very issue. Our OB was resolute in his belief that Doctor D. had been wrong to deliver vaginally and that he had ignored a multitude of warning signs. His deposition testimony sounded so great that I could only wish the jury was already there to hear it. But when, near the very end of the deposition, Bob Clay, representing Pitt Memorial, asked him, "Do you have any criticism of the performance of the nursing staff, particularly the labor and delivery nurses at the hospital?" our obstetrician frankly replied, "The bad outcome was not a result of anything the nurse did or didn't do." He believed that the doctor in charge was the supreme authority.

I tried not to grind my teeth, for it was our belief that what had happened to Jennifer was caused by much more than the failure of any one individual. It was, we were convinced, the result of a systemic problem that involved the entire hospital. The testimony of our OB might establish the responsibility of Doctor D., but at the same time it could destroy the case against the hospital. And our OB was just being courtly: it just didn't seem right, he told us later, to put any blame on nurses, underpaid and underappreciated as they were. I had to respect the man's sentiments. Still, I knew we couldn't bring him with us to Greenville, or Bob Clay would keep him on the stand until he'd convinced every juror to adopt a nurse. We scratched him off our list, which now included only out-of-state physicians who were willing to testify against a North Carolina obstetrician.

Prior to my involvement with the case, Robert Zaytoun had already deposed Doctor D., but for all of Robert's skills, he couldn't lay a glove on the defendant. Doctor D. had a story and he was sticking to it, that Peggy Campbell's situation was perfectly appropriate for a vaginal delivery. Although starting around midafternoon the attending nurse had indeed expressed concerns about what the fetal monitor was registering, the doctor disagreed with her interpretations, then and now. The baby was doing just fine until about ten minutes before her 7:04 P.M. delivery. Up until then, Doctor D. said, he found no "indication that she demanded an urgent delivery." Indications about the baby's condition changed sharply at 6:55 P.M., he testified; but alas, the damage had been instantaneous and irreparable. After four hours of questioning by Robert, Doctor D. left the deposition as unruffled as when he'd begun.

I could only imagine how well he would perform in front of a local jury. Yet there still remained one last way to get at Doctor D., and it was through his own witness, Doctor B.

Doctor B., an expert witness for the defense, had been the supervising physician at Pitt County Memorial Hospital on April 30, 1979. He was an old friend of Doctor D.'s and quite clearly wished to defend him to the death. But he was also a learned man and a very honest one. From studying the considerable evidence, I knew that Doctor D. had been wrong to declare that Jennifer Campbell was doing just fine until 6:55 P.M., when suddenly she was not doing fine. I knew it. I believed Doctor B. knew it. And I believed that I could elicit that judgment from him under oath.

First, I had to become an overnight expert in fetal monitor readings.

An external fetal monitor tracks the progress of a birth on what looks like a wide ticker tape, as it registers the baby's heart rate on one line and the mother's uterine activity or contractions on a line below it. If you stare at the two lines for too long, you go cross-eyed—I did. The expected baseline of a baby's heart rate varies between approximately 120 and 160 beats per minute. A lowering of the heart rate is known as bradycardia, and a rise above the baseline is known as tachycardia. Often a variation from the baseline is explained by what's going on with the mother's contractions, but other deviations not attributable to contractions can point to distress. I had to learn about all of them, and for several evenings prior to my deposing of Doctor B., Elizabeth would wake up in the middle of the night to find me slumped over in a bedroom chair with a medical text on my lap.

I began the March 5, 1985, deposition in Bob Clay's office by asking his expert Doctor B. to render his opinion of our experts. Ours were from out of town, and when it came time for Clay to cross-examine them, he would surely belittle them as hired guns. So I hoped that Clay's own expert would provide them with some cover from Clay's probable attacks by doling out a few collegial compliments to my experts. I wasn't disappointed. "Known to be a reasonable, honest, and competent physician," Doctor B. said of one of our experts. "An honest man who is a good and capable physician and someone I respect," he said of another. So far, so good.

Doctor B.'s basic position was no position at all—that is,

he believed that in 1979, a "significant division in the body of opinion" existed about whether a footling breech baby should be delivered vaginally. As for himself, "I think I probably would not have attempted a double footling breech in 1979." But since he regarded the latter seventies as a "period of transition" in the conventional wisdom, he wouldn't stand in judgment of Doctor D. He didn't offer any evidence of this transition period, nor could he name physicians other than Doctor D. who were then still delivering breech babies vaginally. Nonetheless, Doctor B. had found his comfort zone, a place where he could reconcile his own standards with his affection for Doctor D. And he wouldn't budge from it.

Still, I elicited some potentially useful testimony. Did the Campbells have a right to be informed by Doctor D. or by hospital personnel of the risks associated with vaginal delivery of a breech baby? Yes. Did standards of care vary region by region? "I don't think so. . . . Generally, there is a national standard." (This meant that our out-of-state experts couldn't be impeached by Clay.) Finally, I asked Doctor B. if, based upon his review of the records, he believed that Jennifer's brain damage might have occurred prior to the time Doctor D. ordered emergency delivery. "I know of nothing to suggest that," he replied. This would be the battleground in the case: Were Jennifer's injuries caused during the time Doctor D. ignored evidence of distress and left her in a compromised position in the womb, or was this—as Doctor D. had testified—an instantaneous and irreparable injury that occurred only minutes before he delivered her?

I pulled out the fetal monitor strip. For the next hour, I asked Doctor B. for his interpretation of it, panel by panel. Panel 93080? "There are—that is tracing a heart rate, it varies between about 130 and 150, but it skips in a number of places and is not very clear." Number 93081? "I can't interpret that section very well." And so on—a numbing recitation, until panel 93108. There, the baby's decelerating heartbeat wasn't coinciding with the uterine contraction. "It could be indicative of fetal distress, yes," he acknowledged. Then he hedged. The external monitor reading was almost unintelligible, he said, which is why he himself would have insisted upon attaching a more sensitive internal monitor to the fetus, something that Doctor D. and the attending nurse had failed to do. I saw an opportunity: Would the standards of practice have dictated the use of an internal monitor at that time?

"Yes," he said hesitantly, ". . . yes, I think that's correct."

In panel after panel Doctor B. identified a decelerating heart rate. Panel 93121: "I would consider it compatible with fetal distress." Then, at panel 93124: "I would have taken the baby out." What time did this panel correspond to? 5:30 P.M. And when did Doctor D. indicate the need for urgent delivery? 6:56 P.M.

Doctor B. seemed stunned at his own admission. He again invoked the "period of transition." But I now had on record his statement that from the outset he would have delivered the baby by C-section, and that even had he elected the traditional vaginal-delivery method, the signs of distress evident on the fetal monitor strip would have compelled him to deliver Jennifer fully eighty-six minutes before his friend and colleague did.

Ten days later, on March 15, 1985, Doctor D. settled with the Campbells for $1.5 million.

Now what? It was the Campbells against the hospital, and that was a whole different case. Should we dismiss the suit and move on? No. The hospital's deference to the "captain of the ship" was negligence pure and simple, for the hospital as a whole had a responsibility to Jennifer Campbell and that responsibility had not been met. What if, after seeing the evidence of distress and reporting it to Doctor D., the attending nurse had gone to her supervisor to express her concerns about Doctor D.'s refusal to heed the warnings on the monitor? That supervisor would in turn have reported the matter to Doctor B., the supervising physician—who, we now knew, "would have taken the baby out." Going up the chain of command might have ruffled Doctor D.'s feathers. But it would have saved Jennifer Campbell from irreparable injury. She would be what she had promised to become as late as five o'clock on the afternoon of April 30, 1979—a healthy child.

Although Jeff and Peggy Campbell agreed, they were worried that the legal expenses of trying the case against the hospital would cut into what they'd just won in the settlement for Jennifer's increasingly complicated care. For her sake, a trial was a risk they would rather have avoided, and so at first we did try to avoid it.

Robert Zaytoun approached Bob Clay's associate Alene Mercer with a feeler about settling. He was told the same thing Peter Sarda had been told three years before, when Peter had first offered to dismiss the case against Pitt County Memorial Hospital for $50,000: See you in court.

That was three days away.

• • •

In 1985, if you were born in or near the eastern North Carolina county of Pitt, you were delivered at Pitt County Memorial Hospital. If you suffered any sort of injury or illness, you went to Pitt County Memorial. You could not live in Pitt County without knowing somebody who worked at the hospital. And though it was located on the northwestern periphery of Greenville, its economic and social relevance lay in the dead center of the town's collective consciousness. If I didn't know this before, I sure knew it by jury selection.

A jury of twelve is drawn from a pool of citizens on the county tax rolls and instructed by mail to report for jury duty. Each member of that group is interviewed in a *voir dire* by plaintiff's attorneys and defense attorneys, who jockey to achieve the panel perceived by them to be the most sympathetic to their point of view. Each side can eliminate eight potential jurors without stating a reason. You use one of these "peremptory strikes" to remove someone who, for whatever reason, you believe isn't going to give your client a fair shake. If during *voir dire* you can establish, to the judge's satisfaction, that a member of the jury pool is blatantly and hopelessly biased, you can move that this person be "struck for cause." If the judge agrees, the dismissal of that juror does not count as one of your eight peremptory strikes.

Judges do not strike for cause casually, however. Doctor D.'s wife, had she been in the jury pool, would have been struck for cause. A woman whose baby had been delivered by Doctor D. would not have been—not unless she declared an unwavering loyalty to him. We all have our biases based on our life experiences, so it's unrealistic to imagine a jury free from any prejudice. The question is, can they overcome their prejudice? Will they be fair? Among themselves, can they agree on a decision that metes out justice?

The object of jury selection isn't just to pick a responsive jury, but also to establish a rapport with them during the selection. During *voir dire,* you learn a juror's background. Has he or she suffered any kind of tragedy? What is his or her opinion of doctors, lawyers, insurance companies, and plaintiffs? Would it be unimaginable to punish a hospital or award millions of dollars to the parents of a damaged child, or not award such money for the necessary care of such a child? *Voir dire* is a lawyer's only chance to have a real dialogue with a juror, to challenge his or her attitudes, intellect, and conscience.

Some potential jurors don't want to be chosen for a jury, not in a short case and certainly not in a long one. Even though they have no disqualifying prejudices, they wrangle out of serving, which is usually fine with the lawyers in a long case, who do not want reluctant, impatient jurors, week after week. And some members of the jury pool do want to be chosen, precisely because they do have a bias for one side or because they simply want to be part of a big trial, and so they will try to wrangle their way onto a jury. During *voir dire,* I've seen jurors who want out sidle up to a bias, and I've seen jurors who want to renounce any bias. They are all telling the lawyers something, if only the lawyers will listen. In other words, I have run the gamut of human experience in jury selection. One thing I've never had is a predictable jury—though in Pitt County on Tuesday, March 19, 1985, I feared I would get exactly that.

Not one, not two, not three, but numerous members of the jury pool were employed by or closely related to an employee of the institution that Bob Clay always called "your local hospital." It was all Clay could do to contain his glee as he established the hospital at the heart of the community. One after another, we struck those with close ties to Pitt County Memorial. Those in the pool would titter during my *voir dire,* like an audience in a comedy club that can already see the joke coming: "So you're a housepainter. And what does your wife do for a living, sir?" "She's a secretary." "I see. And where does she work?" "Pitt County Memorial Hospital." And thighs would be slapped as I used up yet another peremptory strike. Bob Clay, on the other hand, had the luxury of striking those jurors who *didn't* have any ties to the hospital.

By the afternoon of Wednesday the twentieth, we had chosen eleven of the twelve jurors. One of them was married to a patient of Doctor D.'s. Others had been treated by Doctor D.'s medical partners. Another was a friend and neighbor of a Pitt County Memorial trustee who had personally recommended that potential juror to Bob Clay. He later became the jury foreman. Every one of the jurors knew the hospital. Not one of them knew Peggy and Jeff Campbell.

We needed only one more juror to fill the jury box, and only one more juror was left in the jury pool. She was a young woman with long hair and a beaded necklace, vaguely hippieish. I asked her if anyone in her family was in the medical profession. "My father," she said.

"And what does he do?"

"He's an obstetrician."

Here we go again, I thought. "And has your father ever been a party to a lawsuit?"

"Yes. He was sued for malpractice."

I couldn't believe it. "Did it have any effect on you personally?"

"Oh, yes. It had an enormous effect on my whole family."

This was obviously a juror we did not want. But we'd used

up all of our peremptory strikes. Our only hope was to have her struck for cause, but the superior court judge would be disinclined to do so for two reasons. First, the woman was the last member left in the pool, and tossing her out would mean an additional one-day delay in the trial so the clerk of court could call up a new pool of potential jurors. Second, the judge had set a low bar for a juror's suitability: he or she needed only to swear to follow the law.

My *voir dire* with this woman lasted well over an hour. I believed there was no way she was going to be fair to us, and I did everything I could to get her to admit it. "You know, ma'am, that I'll be cross-examining a doctor in this trial. And when I do, don't you think it'll remind you of when your own father was cross-examined?"

"I'm sure it will."

"You'll see your dad up there while I'm cross-examining him."

"Probably so."

"And you'll remember what he and your whole family went through."

"Probably, yes."

"And so, don't you at least leave room for the possibility of that having some influence on you?"

"Yes."

"And don't you think that could cause you to lean one way or the other?"

"No."

"No? Ma'am, don't you think if you're actually seeing your father up there on the witness stand, it'll be hard for you to follow the law?"

"No. I'll follow the law."

That was good enough for the judge. But I feared we had a disaster in the making. For several minutes, I pondered whether to use a North Carolina rule that would allow me to dismiss Jennifer's case—and this jury—and refile it within a year. Doing so would delay the suit, which I knew would be excruciating for the Campbells. On the other hand, one juror was all it took to derail our chances.

But who was to say that the next Pitt County jury pool wouldn't be even worse? I left her on, and the jury was impaneled.

Those twelve men and women had two things in common besides their county of residence. Yes, they all knew the defendant and did not know the plaintiffs. But they had seen what that meant as they'd witnessed the stacking up of the odds. Here were working-class parents of a little girl with cerebral palsy alleging damage by the biggest medical system in eastern North Carolina. Jury selection had almost been a dramatization of David and Goliath. The jurors hadn't been asked for any exceptions to be made on behalf of David. But I hoped they would consult their consciences: Does Goliath need our help? Can't we forget our allegiances to this giant and hear what the lawyers for Jennifer Campbell have to say?

•   •   •

In my opening statement I told them, "This lawsuit is not an attack on the nursing profession. Far, far from it. We believe very strongly that what this case is about is an effort to uphold the standards of the nursing profession. . . . You will hear evidence in this case from nurses who make me so proud. They will make you so proud of the nursing profession, you just wouldn't believe. These are women who are willing to stand up and say, 'A nurse has an obligation to the patient—not to the doctor, the doctor's ego. Who cares if you make a doctor mad if a baby is dying in front of your own eyes?' "

Although the attending nurse was not herself a defendant in the lawsuit, Bob Clay had managed to convince the judge to let her, as well as the nurse whose shift had preceded hers on April 30, 1979, sit at the defense table. Although neither of them even worked any longer for Pitt County Memorial Hospital, they sat at the defense table during the trial, and Clay and Mercer referred to them by their first names. Even though the lawsuit was against the hospital, Bob Clay and Alene Mercer's obvious mission was to cast our lawsuit as a vicious assault on these saintly women. We hoped the jurors would see through this charade and conclude that they could not fully trust the picture of the case being drawn by counsel for their local hospital.

Testimony in *Jennifer Campbell v. Pitt County Memorial Hospital* began the following morning with one of our out-of-state medical experts, Dr. Marshall Klavan from Pennsylvania. I looked forward to Dr. Klavan's testimony, and I dreaded the prospect of his cross-examination. He had been an expert witness in dozens of previous trials, a fact I would have to point out to the jury before Bob Clay did. Lawyers love to pounce on "professional witnesses," not only because their testimony seems inherently unreliable, but because, since they sell their expertise, they often buy into their own reputations. Now Dr. Klavan sincerely believed in the merits of our case, but he also believed in himself, and when I met him the evening before his testimony, I tried to get him to scrub off some of that polish, for this was conservative eastern North Carolina, not Philadelphia. Just the evening before I had asked Peggy Campbell to trim the back of my hair so that it wouldn't hang over the collar of my shirt—for Greenville wasn't Raleigh, the state capital, either.

Dr. Klavan, however, simply was and remained slick. He even brought a metal telescopic pointer with him, and when I led him down from the witness stand to explain an exhibit on the easel, Dr. Klavan whipped out his utensil, pushed a button so it would telescope out to an impressive length, and flailed it about like a swordsman. But with each swath, Jennifer's side looked a little less like David.

As an educator, Dr. Klavan was superb. He explained to the jury what a footling breech presentation was, and he described the umbilical cord complications that could occur in a vaginal delivery of a breech baby. He took the jury through Jennifer's fetal monitor reading—his clipped Pennsylvania accent softening as he gave a voice to a clinical apparatus: "What the baby is telling us now is 'I really don't like what's happening to me. I can handle it so far, but you know, I'm going to let you know that something is happening to me.' " What was happening, Dr. Klavan explained, was that the baby was building up an oxygen deficit.

It drove Bob Clay crazy to see Dr. Klavan with his pointer, a real showman and smart as a whip. When Dr. Klavan left the witness stand to use a series of posters to explain to the jury the dangers of a footling breech presentation, Bob Clay had had enough. He interrupted Klavan's anatomy lesson: "I object to the doctor standing in the jury box to give his answer." There was no question about it: to my surprise, the Yankee doctor was scoring big points with this Southern jury. And Bob Clay knew it.

But it was more than that, really: Marshall Klavan was setting the tone for our case, in expert but plainspoken language. "Nurses have fought for a long time to become the professionals they deserve to be," he testified. "As part of their training and responsibility, if they see a situation developing which is going to injure an individual, firstly it is their responsibility to bring that to the attention of the physician. If the physician disagrees with that, it is their responsibility to recognize a life-threatening situation. . . . They have a responsibility to the patient. That's what a hospital is.

"A hospital is not a hotel. A hospital is a refined medical delivery system. A big part of that system is the nursing personnel. If they recognize, as they should, that a baby is in trouble and the physician does not recognize that, they have not only a moral but a professional responsibility to go, as difficult as it may be, up a set chain of command that every hospital administration must insist exist."

Bob Clay's voice dripped with disdain as he cross-examined Klavan. But the Pennsylvania obstetrician gave as good as he got. Wasn't it true that the only time Dr. Klavan had testified in North Carolina it had also been for a plaintiff? Clay was trying to paint him as a doctor who sells his testimony to one side, the plaintiffs. Yes, Dr. Klavan agreed, but in the numerous cases in which he had testified in Pennsylvania, New Jersey, and Delaware, he had testified for the plaintiff patient in about half and for the defendant doctor in about half.

Clay moved on: "Doctor, would you say—if it should develop in the evidence in this case that board-certified OB doctors practicing in hospitals right around here were still doing roughly fifty percent or thereabouts of their footling breech deliveries vaginally in 1979—that they were all practicing below the standard of care?"

Replied Klavan, "Yes, sir. I would. By 1979 one hundred percent of footling breeches should have been delivered by cesarean section."

Bob Clay tried another tack. "Doctor, do you understand the standard of care for physicians to be what they actually are doing, or what you believe they ought to do?"

"Neither. The standard of care is what the majority of good doctors are doing in terms of providing minimal, safe care. And that standard is not set by anything written. It's a reflection of ongoing experiences of various researchers and a reflection of the fact that we talk to each other at meetings from all over the country. We attend the same meetings. We read the same journals. And it's a compilation of all of that, that sets the standard of practice. It's my opinion in 1979, yes, sir, double footling breeches, there was no doubt. They *had* to be delivered abdominally."

Bob Clay was not going to be able to move Dr. Klavan on the standard of care, so he altered course. He got Dr. Klavan to admit that a cesarean delivery is four times more risky for the mother than a vaginal birth. But, of course, Klavan gave him more than Clay wanted. The risk to the baby in the footling breech position increased tenfold in a vaginal delivery over the risk in a C-section, he testified. Then he added, "The risk to the baby is permanent brain damage or death. The risk to mom is a womb infection or other things that antibiotics can deal with."

Klavan was good, but the stars were the nurses. As I have already mentioned, Burton Craige had found four North Carolina nurses willing to testify, and that was no mean feat. They were from Durham, Raleigh, and Greensboro, and none of them had testified before. As Burton and I led each of them through the monitor strips, we could see the jury responding to these women—smart, every bit as capable as the two nurses seated at the defense table, and unequivocal in their belief that the attending nurse should have acted upon the fetal distress signs by consulting a supervisor when Doctor D. failed to heed those signs.

To my relief, Clay and Mercer had not thought to ask our nurses, "Have you ever been convicted of a crime?" Had they done so, they would have discovered that one of our nurses had, in her wild youth, been an SDS radical who had been arrested while protesting the notorious 1968 Democratic National Convention in Chicago. That fact would not have amused our conservative jury and would instead have bolstered the defense's case that, unlike their local nurses, ours were decadent sophisticates who couldn't hope to understand the ways and values of Pitt County.

Instead it was that very former campus radical, now an upstanding nurse, who echoed Marshall Klavan with our most dramatic testimony. "If you can imagine that what we read off of a fetal monitor is the baby's only way to communicate with us," she said as she gestured to the strip, "the baby was saying, 'Help! Help! Let me out!' "

Seated beside Burton at the plaintiff's table, Jeff Campbell burst into tears. Whispering to Peggy, "I can't take this," he tried to contain his sobs as he made his way out of the courtroom.

The witness continued, "When the heart rate falls to less

than ninety [beats a minute], the baby is saying, 'I give up. I quit. Let me out.' "

Clay and Mercer hammered away at the nurses. Were they suggesting that a nurse knew as much as a board-certified obstetrician about fetal distress? Had they ever gone over an OB's head? What did they, big-city nurses, know about the standard of nursing care in Pitt County? And were they aware that each of them disagreed with the other as to precisely when the baby should have been delivered? As it happened, the answers were not identical. But their slight differences of opinion made them seem more authentic, their judgments more genuine. Credibility in the courtroom is made of exactly the same cloth as credibility outside the courtroom.

The defense also brought nurses to the witness stand. Lots of them. Many were from right there in Pitt County—which, as Bob Clay and Alene Mercer would have it, meant that, unlike our city slickers, they could speak realistically as to whether the attending nurse had performed up to the local standard of nursing care. Instead it became apparent that those nurses were towing a company line. They were speaking not as individuals, but rather in a single, unvarying, and well-coached institutional voice.

I elicited an admission from one of the nurses that they had met together for two hours prior to the trial, so it came as no great surprise when, on direct examination, they all said the same thing. A nurse, they all said, should challenge a doctor's wisdom only if he is drunk or belligerent. They all said that although nurses were in fact trained to use fetal monitor strips, obstetricians were better trained to interpret them. Doctor D. was praised up and down by each nurse, and one proclaimed that she trusted him so much that she went to him herself. And naturally, one after another, they held the attending nurse absolutely blameless.

One nurse kept referring to pregnant mothers as "mommies" in her testimony.

"When would you have gotten worried about this baby?" I asked.

"I would have worried the whole time. I mean, the majority of time that I labor a mommy, I'm concerned. It doesn't matter what presentation she's in," she said, somewhat sensibly, I thought. But she continued, gushing, "I love my mommies and babies." I wanted to find out how far that love might go, and so on cross-examination I took her through a series of hypothetical situations—each of which had actually occurred on April 30, 1979—and I then asked her what she herself would have done. If she had seen signs of variable deceleration on the monitor, brought them to the doctor's attention, and the doctor did nothing, what would she have done?

Well, she replied, she would try to keep the mommy comfortable and would keep watching the fetal monitor.

And if she had seen signs of bradycardia—the depression in the baby's heart rate—and informed the doctor, and still he did nothing, what would she do?

Well . . . keep the mommy comfortable and keep watching the monitor.

In other words, she would defer to the doctor at all times.

"And you'd stand there and watch the baby die," I said.

"Objection!" said Bob Clay.

"Sustained," said Judge Phillips. But I'd made my point.

Another of Clay's nurses was more adamant, even strident,

about the deference afforded a doctor. "I have never known a nurse to question a physician," she proclaimed to Burton on cross-examination. "I have never talked to a nurse that has gone through the so-called chain of command. . . . Yes, I have been in a situation when I did not think [the doctor] was intervening [in response to fetal distress], and what did I do? Nothing. And I've never known a nurse that has done anything other than that in that situation." So it was her testimony that the standard of care was that a nurse watching evidence of fetal distress would do nothing? "Yes," she testified, "as long as the physician is in the room."

Burton pressed her: What about in an ominous situation like bradycardia, which can signal impending fetal death?

"Obviously that does not apply in this case," she snapped, "because you did not get a dead baby, right?"

As soon as the words crossed her lips, the temperature in the courtroom must have dropped thirty degrees. Burton let the nurse's callous retort hang in the air for a moment before saying, "No further questions."

Slowly, witness by witness, I could see that the message was getting through to the jury: the "captain of the ship" credo was antiquated, wrongheaded, and dangerous. I actually felt sorry for the attending nurse when, during my cross-examination, she tried to defend both herself and Doctor D. in their contradictory opinions of Jennifer Campbell's heart rate.

Other witnesses had testified that the nurse and Doctor D. were both in the room with Peggy from 5:00 P.M. until she went to the delivery room nearly two hours later. By 5:23 P.M., the nurse testified that she "was concerned that there were variable decelerations on the monitor strip that indicated cord compression." At 5:31, again at 5:35, and at 5:39, she noted other decelerations and told Doctor D. "I don't recall his response," she said, but there was no change in the way Doctor D. treated his patient. So at 5:55 P.M. she listened for the baby's heartbeat with a fetoscope, with which she could detect "a well-defined variable deceleration." Then she would hand the instrument over to Doctor D. "He would say, 'It's coming back up,' and he was satisfied with the rate that it was coming back up to. . . . He was reassuring that what he was hearing was okay."

I persisted. Was she saying Doctor D. had a better reading of the fetal heart rate than she did? Of course that was what Doctor D. himself had contended. But the nurse knew that wasn't true. She had faithfully and accurately recorded Jennifer's decline.

"So he was telling you during this time, beginning at six P.M., that his readings were better, I guess, than the readings you were getting, is that fair?"

"No," she answered. "He was saying—I was saying at the time I heard it was what I was documenting, and he was saying what he heard when he was listening. It's not that it's better. It's just that that's the pattern we were getting."

The absurdity of this explanation was embarrassing. From 6:07 P.M. on for nearly an hour, every single fetoscope reading she made was in bradycardia range. And according to Doctor D., every single fetoscope reading he made was in the normal range. "Do you believe," I asked gently, "that during that one-hour period, you happened to listen to the heart rate every time when it was down, and Doctor D. happened to listen to it every time it went up?"

But the most articulate spokesperson about the spoken and unspoken power of a physician was another Pitt County nurse.

On direct examination, she echoed the testimony of her colleagues. When I cross-examined her, I asked if she had ever gone to a supervisor to register her concern about a physician's approach to a patient. When she replied that she had, I asked her to tell us about the experience.

"It's a pretty sticky situation when you have to contact other people about the care that a patient is receiving," she said. "Because you are questioning whether you feel that a doctor is competent or not. And that really steps on his toes in a real big way. You're really taking a very big risk as a nurse to do that because you stand a real good chance of losing your job on the spot if it's a doctor that has considerable power—which most doctors have, considerable power."

The nurse's reply—unvarnished, heartfelt—was direct and honest. And the jury knew it. I almost didn't know what to ask next.

"Is that something that you would worry about if you were doing that kind of thing?" I managed.

"Definitely," she said.

"You'd worry about your job."

"Definitely."

• • •

I mentioned earlier that Doctor D. was not at all like the Asheville doctor who had treated E.G. Sawyer. Doctor D. was genial, calm, caring, sure-handed, and wise. He even looked like a doctor, a modern Marcus Welby from the 1970s television series, like a doctor you or I might want by our bedside. Doctor D. was, without question, a good man. Never for a moment had I thought otherwise.

But time was beginning to pass him by. Our expert, Marshall Klavan, had it right: in medicine, the standard of care is not static. It evolves with continuing research, new technologies, and advances in pharmacology. While by 1979 his colleagues had come to see the virtues of cesarean deliveries for high-risk pregnancies, Doctor D. had not. His stubbornness, combined with the attending nurse's deference to him, had needlessly caused a tragedy on April 30, 1979. For all his fine traits, Doctor D. had been flat wrong on the medicine. And that was what I intended to show the jury on Good Friday, when Doctor D. took the stand.

Because another big trial was taking place in the courthouse, ours was moved to a different courtroom that was so small and muggy that the bailiff had opened all the windows. The gray-haired Doctor D. had performed ably under direct examination from Bob Clay—folksy and at the same time authoritative, and I could see that he was winning the jury's collective heart as he testified. If the defense's previous witnesses had sounded rehearsed and almost inhuman, Doctor D. was inarguably the real deal. Here was a reason to side with "your local county hospital."

Under direct examination, Doctor D. had cited a statistic that, in 1979, fully 52 percent of all breech babies at Pitt County Memorial had been delivered vaginally. I began my cross-examination with that rather startling number. Did that statistic include both footling and frank (bottom-first) presentations? It did, he acknowledged. Weren't frank babies a great deal more common than footling babies? They were, he admitted. And didn't footling babies run a far greater risk of a prolapsed umbilical cord than frank babies? They did, he agreed. The last point was important because when the umbilical cord drops beneath or between the baby's legs, it can become compressed and the oxygen supplied through the cord to the baby and importantly the baby's brain can be dangerously compromised. Jennifer was born with the umbilical cord wrapped tightly around her legs.

I asked Doctor D. if he considered the universally respected textbook *Williams Obstetrics* to be an authoritative text. He said he did. I then asked if he agreed with the following passage from that book: "To try to minimize infant mortality and morbidity, cesarean section is now commonly used in the following circumstances to deliver all but the very immature fetus: footling breech presentation."

"No, I would not agree with that," he replied.

Did he agree with the book's assertion that the incidence of umbilical cord prolapse is twenty times greater for breech babies than nonbreech babies? After hedging, he replied, "I wouldn't disagree with that, no."

During Clay's examination, Doctor D. had expressed admiration for the works of Dr. Kenneth R. Niswander, so I read from one of Niswander's 1976 texts: "Recently, increasing numbers of obstetricians are recommending and practicing cesarean section of virtually all patients with breech presentation. Those opposed to routine cesarean section advocate vaginal delivery for the breech presentation, with the following exceptions: footling presentations, because of the substantial risk of umbilical cord prolapse."

"I don't believe that holds true in the general areas of community practice," Doctor D. replied.

"But," I said, "this is the same Dr. Niswander that you were referring to in response to Mr. Clay's questions, is that right?"

"I presume it is," he said. "I'm not familiar with that article."

And so it went for hours as the weight of medical opinion was stacked against him, until Doctor D. stood alone in disagreement with his friends and colleagues. Finally, I asked him about Jeff Campbell's recollection that Doctor D. had said he felt a scrotum between the baby's legs. In his deposition a year before, he had emphatically denied making that comment.

"I guess what I need to know about that is whether you would deny making such a statement," I said, "or whether you just don't remember."

Doctor D.'s fatigue was palpable.

"I don't remember making that statement," he said.

And would a prolapsed umbilical cord wrap itself between the baby's legs?

Yes, he acknowledged.

And as the mother progressed through labor, would that cord become increasingly tighter, cutting off oxygen?

It might, he conceded.

That was as close as Doctor D. came to admitting that he had felt with his very own hand the tragedy that was enfolding for Jennifer Campbell on the afternoon of April 30, 1979, and that he simply hadn't seen it for what it was. But now he appeared to see it—and so, I hoped, did the jury.

· · ·

Today I give speeches on the Senate floor much as I presented my closing arguments as a trial lawyer. I don't read from a prepared text. Instead, I organize a body of ideas and then distill them down to a short series of points that I write out on a piece of paper, barely legible, even to myself. This approach doesn't always yield the most flowing rhetoric, but it allows me to speak to the jurors from the heart. The struggle to earn and keep credibility begins the first time that the jury sees you, and it does not end until the jury door closes. An artful and beautifully constructed closing argument read from a sheaf of papers is, in my view, just like the defense's parade of nurses each reciting the same speech. The perfection of it was alluring but it does not have the ring of truth to it. If I spoke directly and plainly to the jury, I could convey, however imperfectly, what I truly believed. And that is what I needed to do.

I had all of Easter weekend to prepare my closing, and I didn't sleep much. A good closing argument should embody all of the trial's most telling moments, and I felt them all roiling inside me as I sat in a hotel room crammed with trial exhibits, medical literature, legal notepads, and half-eaten food, all pretty much in disarray, just as I was.

I kept returning to the fetal monitor strip and to the tracings that represented Jennifer's heartbeat. We had shown the strip to over a dozen witnesses—from Dr. Klavan, the very first, to Doctor D., the very last. The defense had not done so even once, in part because it was, after all, the voice of Jennifer. The jury would need to understand that.

Then there was Jennifer herself. Now just a few weeks shy of her sixth birthday, the little girl had not once set foot in the Greenville courtroom. We knew that her presence would appear to be tugging at the jury's heartstrings, with all the positives and negatives that triggered. Still, this was her case and her life, and those twelve men and women needed to see her. So we composed and introduced into evidence a thirty-minute "day in the life" video. In it, Jennifer struggled to ride her tricycle, to put on her sweater, to eat. She persevered with great effort, always assisted by her wonderfully patient parents, and was never discouraged by failure. There was nothing high-gloss about the videotape. But its message was powerful: this was a courageous little girl.

And now the jury was almost ready to weigh her case against the most powerful medical entity in eastern North Carolina. Weeks before in *voir dire,* the jurors had told the judge how they'd been born at Pitt County Memorial Hospital, how their sisters had worked there, their fathers had been treated there. Every member of that jury knew how important this hospital was to this community and to the entire eastern part of the state. They would need courage in deciding Jennifer's case, and I would ask them for that courage.

Monday morning began with Robert Zaytoun summarizing our case to the jury. Above all he sought to assuage the concern that a verdict might destroy or even harm the two neatly dressed nurses sitting at the defense table. "As representatives of this hospital, they just didn't do enough to protect the patients that they had, and that's why they are involved," Robert said. "But they will walk away from this case after it's over. They will think about the result, but it will not have any direct bearing on them, financially or otherwise."

But in her closing, Alene Mercer, who had been a nurse before she started law school with Elizabeth and me in 1974, kept the focus on the nurses, and she did so brilliantly. Her nurses were experienced and dedicated, while our nurses, she said, were hardly qualified to judge what the standard of care was in Pitt County. And Bob Clay's closing was skillful, although he could not resist dispensing a left-handed compliment to our side: "Well, they've done a real good job of making bricks without straw."

Alene Mercer had ended with a prediction about my closing: "I fully expect that while you hear Mr. Edwards arguing to you, he will have most of you in tears by the time he's done," she said. "I suspect we'll all be affected by his argument. I plan on having my box of Kleenex ready."

And so I began. "There's an advantage to going last. . . . But there's also a disadvantage. And the disadvantage is this: I'm worried that some of you have already made up your minds before I ever stand up. And if that's true, you're not being fair."

I stared at the twelfth juror, the obstetrician's daughter. She would not look at me.

"There's one part of these arguments that really bothers me," I went on. "And it was part of Ms. Mercer's argument. She told you at the end of her argument that I would stand before you and I would have you all in tears. Well, first of all, she gives me more credit than I deserve."

Still nothing from the obstetrician's daughter. I continued, "But what I want to say to you is, what I do intend to do is be straight with you. And I'll tell you now that there is no emotion attached to the first three issues in this case, and you should decide those issues without passion, without prejudice for or against Jennifer Campbell. Those are issues that have to be decided simply based on the evidence.

"Now, the last three issues . . . are the damages issues. Those issues are emotional. I can't make them not emotional. There's nothing I can do about that. I'm going to try to be as fair and honest and straight with you on those issues as I will be on the first three issues, but I don't promise you that those issues won't be emotional, because they will be."

I turned to a remark that Bob Clay had made in his closing about how rigorous the jury selection process had been for this trial. "Well, it was hard," I said. "And it was difficult. But not"—I gestured toward Clay—"for *this* side. Those of you who were there in the beginning and sat through the whole process, I want you to think back. How many people knew Peggy Campbell, and how many people knew Jeff Campbell, and how many people ever heard of Jennifer Campbell? And then I want you to remember how many people knew Doctor D., and how many people had relatives who had worked at, or *they* worked at, Pitt County Memorial Hospital?" I went on, "All the fancy talk in the world doesn't change what this lawsuit is. This lawsuit is a couple from Winterville, North Carolina, and a six-year-old girl against the largest hospital in eastern North Carolina. That's what it is."

The economic and civic importance of Pitt County Hospital to the entire region was—and is—enormous. And I knew it would be hard for the jury to decide against the hospital, just as it was difficult for nurses in the state to testify against the hospital. I turned to the nurses. According to both Mercer and Clay, our nurses were straight-from-the-ivory-tower, untrustworthy witnesses. I said that characterization was unfair. "I want you to think about if you were sitting over here, regular people from a small town in eastern North Carolina, trying to find nurses, good, credible nurses, who will walk into a courtroom, get on that witness stand, and testify against the most powerful hospital in eastern North Carolina. . . . And then I want you to think about the courage, the courage this required, for a nurse to come down here, get on this witness stand in Greenville, North Carolina, the hometown of this hospital, and testify against the hospital. What did those four nurses have to gain from this? What, in heaven's name, what reason did they have to be here?

"You have got to put this case in perspective. You must understand the imbalance that you're confronted with when you're on this side. Mr. Clay told you that he's been doing this for a long time, and he has, and he's very good at it. Well, I haven't been doing it nearly as long as him. But what I do is, I do what I'm doing in this case. I represent people."

And yet, I said, for all of the defense's corporate might, its contention that Doctor D. had performed in accordance with the standard of care had no evidentiary support. "Now, if that were true—use your common sense—if that were true, can you imagine the parade of board-certified obstetricians that would have gotten on that stand for the defendant and said it? Doctor D. knows every obstetrician in eastern North Carolina. Where are they? Where were they? We saw one . . . his partner, practiced with him for forty years; and even he couldn't come very far.

"The bottom line is, Doctor D. is not an evil person. My judgment of Doctor D.—you've got to make your own judgment—is that he is a quality person . . . but on April 30, 1979, having been in the hospital for twelve hours, he was wrong. It's as simple as that. He's human, he makes mistakes, and he was wrong on that day. And that's why the hospital is there."

I turned to the factual issues in the case. Did Pitt County Memorial, as an accredited hospital, honor its legal obligation to inform the patient of the risks associated with vaginally delivering a footling breech baby? The defense had all but conceded that Peggy Campbell had never been warned about the possibility of a prolapsed umbilical cord. The hospital's obligation was stated in the manual of the organization that accredited hospitals: "The patient has the right to reasonably informed participation in decisions involving his health care. This should be based on a clear, concise, explanation of his condition and of all proposed technical procedures, including the possibilities of any risk of mortality or serious side effects." The Campbells had neither been informed about the risks of a footling breech presentation nor had they consented to a vaginal delivery before Jennifer's birth. But Jeff had been asked to sign an "informed consent" statement after the delivery. The hospital had, of course, dismissed the significance of the fact that Jeff Campbell was not asked to sign the consent form until eighty-four minutes after Jennifer's birth.

"Well, there are a couple of things I'd say to you about that," I said. "First, if that consent form had been signed at two in the afternoon, I wouldn't be the one talking about it. *They* would. They would be waving that consent form all over this courtroom . . . 'They consented. Look, they signed the form.'

"Second point is, although it 'doesn't matter,' it's 'not significant,' 'not important,' it mattered enough within an hour after this baby was born with brain damage that Doctor D. and the nurse wanted Jeff Campbell's signature on that form. . . . I suggest to you that the only reasonable inference from that is, they got in there, they saw what happened with this baby, and they said, 'We've got a problem. These people were never told about any of this. Let's get their signature on a consent form.' " And I reminded the jury that even when the nurse got Jeff Campbell's signature on the informed consent statement, she still did not give him information he should have had: his daughter was suffering from near terminal depression and she was barely hanging on to life. What did she tell him? That mother and baby were doing fine. And in response to some of their nurses' testimony that sometimes there is no time to get a signature on a consent form, I knew the jury could tell there was time in Jennifer's case, so I simply said, "There's no evidence that they *tried* to do what they're required to do."

I conceded that the most difficult issue in the case concerned the nurses' negligence. It was difficult legally, and it was difficult emotionally. Fully ten nurses, theirs as well as ours, had acknowledged that when a patient's health is threatened, the nurse has a duty to do whatever is necessary to treat that patient. "Was there a threat to the health of Jennifer Campbell?" I asked. "If there was, the duty exists."

There was plenty of evidence that Jennifer's health was at risk on the afternoon of April 30, 1979, but I needed to make sure that the jury understood it. And I needed to show that the nurses had understood it when they saw it. Bob Clay had been dismissive about our continual reliance on the fetal monitor strips. "We sighed along with you every time the strips got brought out," he had said, subtly aligning himself with the jury. Maybe the strips were tedious, I admitted, but the truth was in those strips. "Six years ago was when all this happened. People don't remember everything that happened. But those strips don't lie." I flipped through the list of witnesses. "One, two, three, four, five, six, seven, eight, nine, ten witnesses were shown the strips. Ten witnesses said: fetal tachycardia, variable decelerations, variable decelerations with a slow return, bradycardia, periodic bradycardia . . . By five-thirty every sign of fetal hypoxia, every sign of a problem was there by five-thirty." Ten witnesses had identified the deprivation of oxygen to Jennifer's brain.

Only one did not: Doctor D. And he was flat wrong.

"He was just wrong. Everybody makes mistakes. [T]here was a safety valve there," I continued, gesturing to the nurses still seated with Clay and Mercer, "but it didn't work." Had it not worked because she agreed with Doctor D.? Had it not worked simply because she didn't recognize the problem? In Jennifer's case, the attending nurse "not only should have recognized the problem, she did." In the labor room, she "saw what nine other people saw" when they read the strips in the courtroom. She called Doctor D. at 5:15 "because she knew this baby was in trouble." She saw Jennifer's distress, and when Doctor D. did nothing about it, she also did nothing. Had she gone up the chain of command, the supervising physician, Doctor B., would have, by his own deposition testimony, "gotten that baby out."

The third issue for the jury to decide concerned corporate negligence. I reminded the jury of the surprise testimony of the defense's own nurse when she said that if she challenged a physician's judgment she risked being fired.

"Now, you tell me whose responsibility it is to ensure that those nurses, and everybody else who works at the hospital, know that they can do what has to be done, and they'll be protected," I said. "That is the hospital's responsibility. It's not the nurses' responsibility." Dr. Klavan had said it best: the hospital was not a hotel.

Furthermore, I said that the responsibility of ensuring that Peggy and Jeff Campbell were given sufficient information for informed consent did not end with Doctor D. For an accredited medical institution, "The law requires that the hospital oversee the treatment. And the hospital does not walk away from that obligation because the doctor is standing there. That obligation is there all the time, under the law."

At last I came to the issue of damages. The "special damages"—those for lifetime health-care expenses and lost wages—though staggering, were fairly cut and dry. The "general damages," referring to Jennifer's suffering, were far harder to calculate. Rather than assign some big, abstract number to what her life would be like, I spoke of each element of damage individually. The loss of the use of her legs. Her permanent brain damage. The partial loss of manual dexterity. Her disfigurement. Her severely impaired speech. The physical pain and suffering from having to undergo several more surgeries. And finally, the emotional suffering Jennifer would have to endure as a consequence of the hospital's negligence.

"Jennifer's six years old now, and she's cute—she's a wonderful little girl," I said. "The problem is this, that you see her now and you think that's what her life is going to be: she's disabled, but everybody adores her. Well, that's true when you're six. But five years from now, she'll be eleven. And at age eleven she'll have had a chance to experience the cruelty of other children. . . . When she's in her twenties, her sister will be getting married, her sister will be going off to college. Jennifer will be home. . . . Thirty years from now, Jennifer will be a thirty-six-year-old. She'll be working in a sheltered workshop, her life will be a life composed of braces, walkers. . . . Forty years from now, fifty years from now, when she's fifty years old, fifty-six years old, nobody will remember that sweet, cute six-year-old little girl. Fifty-six-year-old women with cerebral palsy are not so cute anymore."

It was crass, I acknowledged, to assign a dollar figure to these matters. But it was the jury's duty to do so. "There is no higher calling than to sit on a jury in a case this important," I said. "And you have a chance in this case to have such an impact on the life of Jennifer Campbell. Even more importantly than that, you have a chance to send a message in this case that can't fail to be understood.

"But I'll say this to you. If you come back in this case either with a verdict for the defendant or with a smaller verdict . . . the message you will have will be clear and it will be plain, and that is: 'Hospital, we will not hold you responsible. We will say to you, you are a hotel. You have no responsibility other than that.'

"And you will put your stamp of approval not only on what happened here but what will happen from this day forward. All I can say to you about that is, if that's what you want, and that's what you want your verdict to be in this case, I only hope to God you're sure that doctors don't make mistakes. Because I'm here to tell you that they do. And I'm not the only one who's telling you that. Doctor D. told you that. And you've got to take that into consideration.

"You know, six years ago, Jennifer Campbell did everything she knew how to do on the afternoon of April thirtieth, 1979, to speak to the hospital, and the only way she knew how to do it was through that strip. And what she said to them is this. She said at three, 'I'm fine.' She said at four, 'I'm having a little bit of trouble, but I'm doing okay.' Five, she said, 'I'm having problems.' At five-thirty, she said, 'I need out.'

"And she said it to everyone there. At then at six, the cries got weaker. . . . And the cries they heard were the cries of Jennifer Campbell dying. . . . But she didn't die. She made it. She survived, and she's been fighting every way she knows how since.

"And so here we are again. She speaks to you again. But now she speaks to you, not through a fetal monitor strip; she speaks to you through me. And I have to tell you right now—I didn't plan to talk about this—right now I feel her, I feel her presence; she's inside me, and she's talking to you. This is her. What I'm saying to you is what Jennifer Campbell has to say to you.

"And this is what she says to you. She says, 'I don't ask for your pity. What I ask for is your strength. And I don't ask for your sympathy, but I do ask for your courage. I ask you to do what I've done for the last six years. I ask you to be courageous.' "

My thoughts slipped then—as they had so many times in this trial—to my own son, born just weeks after Jennifer. Wade had been learning to read in kindergarten, and while I was in Greenville he had labeled all the furniture in his room with their names—or something resembling their names. He had a small speech impediment, and so each of the drawers was labeled with the name he used: *jars*. Elizabeth and I laughed about it, which we could do because we knew this was a minor hurdle before a future of opportunity. How different Jennifer's prospects were from Wade's.

I went on, "I've got a five-year-old boy who is almost the same age as Jennifer, and I can't look at him now without thinking about her. And I can only hope and pray to God that my boy will have the strength that Jennifer Campbell has. That's the best I could ever hope for him.

"And what she asks of you is to have the same courage that she has, no matter what the consequences, to do what the law requires in this case. The word *verdict—verdict* is a Latin word and what it means is this: it means to speak the truth. Jennifer Campbell asks you to let your verdict speak the truth in this case. She asks you to take this burden that she's carried for six years off of Peggy and Jeff Campbell and off of Jennifer, and to put it where it belongs.

"Six years ago, her cries were not answered. And I refuse to believe that that's going to happen in this courtroom again tomorrow."

During my closing arguments I kept my eyes on the jury. But Robert Zaytoun watched the judge. And he thought he saw in Judge Phillips's normally expressionless face a flash of something new—a sudden awareness that something big, and maybe enormous, was unfolding in his courtroom. Whatever the shortcomings of my closing arguments, they were certainly deeply felt, and it may be that the judge had suddenly come to distrust the force with which they seemed to be hitting the jury. Robert sensed trouble from the judge, and in fact there would be trouble in a few weeks.

But for the moment it was my last chance to describe, in simple terms that meant something to the jury of regular people, the terrible thing that had really happened. It was the last chance to make clear or try to translate what great negligence had meant to Jennifer Campbell—that now she had cerebral palsy, that now she required constant care and constant supervision and would always need it. The litany of her injuries was striking. At delivery she had sustained brain damage due to severe asphyxia from the entangled cord, she had suffered a fractured right clavicle and extreme general blood anoxia, and she had been left with neurological residual motor deficiency and static perinatal encephalophy manifested by spastic quadroperisis with a diplegic patter. There had been psychomotor retardation, neonatal seizures, and bilateral metatarsis abductis, and all of this was complicated by the brain trauma she had suffered due to forceful application of metal forceps to her emerging head.

The jury began its deliberations on the morning of Wednesday, April 10. By the end of the afternoon, the foreman announced that they would need more time.

Thursday morning the jury reconvened, and the hours crept by. Those hours can be torture for a lawyer, for you sit there in the near empty courtroom, surrounded by stacks of briefs, texts, depositions, exhibits, and notepads, and none of them are of any use except to remind you of the things you might have said better and all the things you might have done differently.

You try to visualize each juror and imagine what each of them will bring to the deliberations. I had obsessed over the obstetrician's daughter throughout the trial, and I could not shake the idea that she might now be trying to recruit other jurors against the Campbells.

At that point your clients are similarly helpless. You want to exude confidence when you are around them, but much of the time it's they who are comforting you, and assuring you that you've done a fine job—which only deepens your fear that you have failed such good people. I certainly felt that way about Jeff and Peggy Campbell. Still barely more than kids, of course, they had never been through anything like this before. But if some of the more complex legal questions eluded them, a fundamental fact did not: the Campbell family was going to survive. Jeff and Peggy were going to devote their lives to taking care of Jennifer whether or not the jury held the hospital accountable for its negligence. No matter what happened, it would never be easy for them. Many people waiting for that verdict—court officers, the press, witnesses—saw the young couple praying in the courthouse hallway, and I saw them too. In my own way, I prayed that I had not let them down.

At 12:30 in the afternoon of April 11, we rose from our seats as the jury filed back in the courtroom. We all watched their faces.

"Would you hand the verdict to the bailiff, please?" the judge asked the foreman.

The foreman did so. The bailiff, in turn, handed the sheet to the judge.

He stared at it. Then he moved it farther from his face and squinted. Then he brought the sheet toward him again.

"Would the clerk take the verdict," he said quietly.

"Will you please stand, ladies and gentlemen," said the clerk of the court. The jurors rose to their feet.

"Ladies and gentlemen of the jury. You have answered the first question"—Were the plaintiffs injured by the negligence of the nurses?—"No."

My heart seized up. We'd lost the first issue.

"The second issue"—Were the plaintiffs injured by the defendant Pitt County Memorial Hospital's failure to insure the plaintiffs' informed consent had been obtained?—"Yes."

"The third issue"—were the plaintiffs injured by the corporate negligence of the defendant, Pitt County Memorial Hospital?—"Yes."

And then the clerk listed the damages to be awarded to the Campbells. They totaled $6.5 million.

Alene Mercer flung her head into her arms.

The judge remained seated in his chair well after he'd declared the court adjourned.

And I hugged the Campbells, and we felt great relief and joy that their long fight for justice was over.

But it was not.

• • •

I don't know how to account for what went on in the judge's mind between the time of the verdict on April 11, 1985, and the post-trial motions conference five weeks later. But as I have suggested, I am convinced that he had been caught unawares by what he saw coming together in his courtroom during my closing argument. Before he knew it, the jury had returned a record-breaking verdict, one that other judges—and many other people—would surely question him about. Headlines on nearly all newspapers in the eastern part of the state trumpeted the record. Conversations in Greenville revolved around the verdict. It all might well have made him uneasy and might well have given rise to some gnawing suspicion that something too extraordinary and not quite right had taken place under his watch and that, inadvertently, he had let it happen.

And so, on May 17, 1985, the judge pleasantly informed us that he was setting the verdict aside. He believed that it was "excessive and appears to have been given under the influence of passion and prejudice, and the evidence was insufficient to support the verdict." Instead, he announced, he would award Jennifer precisely half of the damages that the jury, after weeks of trial and hours of deliberation, had determined fair. We could voluntarily accept the reduced award, or he would order a new trial.

"*What?*"

I had never been angrier in my entire life. "What did we sit in that courtroom for three weeks for?" I demanded. "Are *you* the jury?"

"John," said Judge Phillips gently, "you need to calm down."

"No! I don't need to calm down! This is about a child's life—and you've just taken this verdict away from her!"

But the judge had decided upon his remedy and he would not be moved from it.

Robert, Burton, and I drove to Winterville in silence. Jeff and Peggy Campbell's faces fell as soon as they saw ours. I think I had expected them to be outraged as we had been, to rail as we had railed, but I'll never forget their reaction. We'll do whatever you think is right, they said. We're used to going through tough times. We have faith that it'll work out.

Their serenity—I don't know any other word to describe it—might have calmed me, but it didn't. I was even more determined that the Campbells would not lose before a judge what they had won before a jury.

And we didn't lose. We turned down the judge's remittitur of damages, and he promptly ordered a new trial on the damages question. We appealed the judge's decision—a formidable task, since in North Carolina a judge's ruling can only be overturned if it's found that he abused his discretion. For the next two and one half years, the case wrangled its way through the appellate courts.

On February 17, 1988, Pitt County Memorial Hospital finally agreed to settle the case with the Campbells for $4.25 million. The sum ensured that Jennifer, now nearly nine, would be taken care of for the rest of her life.

• • •

The Campbell verdict set in motion a wave of reforms throughout the North Carolina medical community. Almost overnight, as we learned, hospital board members ratified procedures through which personnel could go up a chain of command to protect a patient's welfare. Hospital nurses later reported to us that they were empowered by the reforms. Hospitals would be stronger now, and safer. On the legal front, *Jennifer Campbell v. Pitt County Memorial Hospital* made case law on the issue of informed consent: a hospital could now be held liable if it failed to ascertain whether a patient understood the various risks associated with a medical procedure.

After the headlines stopped, I could take some satisfaction in the changes I saw happening in hospitals, the empowering of nurses, the new, stricter requirements about informed consent. But in the end this was always a case about one family. When my hometown newspaper called about the importance of the verdict, I told them that first this case was about a six-year-old girl and her parents, good working people. Because it was.

And when the case was over, I returned to my life in Raleigh, to my family. My daughter Cate was now three, the same age Jennifer had been when I'd first met her. As I sat in the amphitheater at the Rose Garden in Raleigh that spring, I watched Cate in pink tights, leaping and twirling with her classmates at Arts Together, but I could not forget the image of Jennifer, struggling at three to master standing at that startling corner feeder in her playpen. And she mastered it. And I thought: there is, in this world, more than one form of grace.

JOSH

WHEN I WAS A BOY, it became a ritual for my father and me to drive to Clemson University on autumn Saturdays to watch the Tigers play. My father would plunk down the change for general-admission seats, and the cashier would slide over two orange tickets, and then a minute later we would be engulfed in a sea of orange sweatshirts and banners. After the game we would hang back in the parking lot and watch the players file out of the stadium. Although my dad had never been able to attend college, he had been raised in the shadow of Clemson— whose football team he loved. Clemson University was the missed dream for him, and it was a missed dream he pretty much circled around whenever he drove to work or anywhere else in that part of the state. I couldn't have been more than eleven or twelve when I first came to understand how much he must have regretted his missed chance of college—and maybe even of playing football. I got it into my head that I might give him some part of his fantasy, or at least I hoped I could. I knew it would mean a lot to him if he could see his son among the ranks at that school, and maybe even out on the field. And that became my plan.

I worked hard in high school, and I practiced football. At North Moore High School the success I had as a starting receiver was the result of thousands of passes my dad had flung in my direction in our front yard in Robbins. If I caught a touchdown pass for North Moore, or if I dropped one, the first person I looked to was my dad. And he would be there, in heat and rain, sitting on the pine bleachers, up high where he would be certain to see everything. He and my mother were at every basketball game and every track meet. It was not complicated. We were family, and we were friends.

I had other friends of course, but since we moved around so much when I was young, my parents were the only constant presence in my life. I once assumed that our friendship was mainly due to their having been so young when they got married, my mother only eighteen and my father nineteen, so my dad was only forty and my mother was only thirty-nine when I was twenty years old—mama used to say we grew up together. But at the root of our friendship, my parents taught me something deeper—and it had to do with mutual respect. Elizabeth and I were already thirty and twenty-six when our first son Wade was born, and it is a glorious fact that Elizabeth was fifty when she had our beautiful son Jack. Although we are much older parents than Bobbie and Wallace Edwards were, it is absolutely true that our children are our friends and we are theirs. Elizabeth and I are grateful for having been taught how that can happen.

When I made the freshman team as a walk-on wide receiver at Clemson, my parents often made the drive from Robbins to watch me play. But my slim success as a college player was a far cry from what it had been in high school when my dad's friends would slap him on the back and say something that always seemed to start, "That boy of yours . . ." Since I wasn't big enough to play for a top-level college team, I soon realized that I was unlikely to make varsity and so I was not going to get the athletic scholarship I needed to continue at Clemson. So after only one semester I had to leave the school that meant so much to both me and my family. I wasn't used to failure, and I was miserable that I had failed my dad.

But as unhappy as that time was, the bad things have mostly fallen away. What I really remember is where I lived during those few months, and I remember the best parts of my days at Clemson. My maternal grandmother, Grandma Pauline, had a small house in the mill village of next-door Seneca, and so I stayed with her during that one semester—the football player and his grandma. What comes back to me is simple—getting up in the morning and having breakfast together and my attempts to get the heater started. And then sitting with her in the living room in the evening, me studying while she watched me with my textbooks and my mysterious pads of paper. Who knows what she was thinking, but she made me feel safe. I was, she would tell me, the apple of her eye. In many ways it was the worst time in the life of that eighteen-year-old boy, but it was a very fine time for him too.

Partly because I had to leave Clemson, I am now so grateful that I can send my own children to college. Until I began at Clemson in the fall of 1971—and then NC State in Raleigh and law school at the University of North Carolina at Chapel Hill—no one in my family, not my parents or my grandparents, or my great-grandparents, or anyone as far back as I knew, had even attended college, much less graduated, and few had even considered the possibility. None of my four smart grandparents had even finished high school—which for them, as for so many of their generation and my parents' generation, was a luxury not all people could afford.

We were a mill family. My father worked in Milliken's textile plants for thirty-six years. My mother started her work life in the mills, sewing sheets and bathing suits. Her own mother had spun yarns in the mills, and my dad's mom had been a weaver. At the time of my birth in Seneca, South Carolina, in 1953, my parents lived in a three-room, white wood-frame cottage in the Utica "mill village"—a neighborhood where the company owned all the houses and rented them out to the employees in the town's mills. Whenever we relocated—and we did so five times before I was twelve—it was always a move required by the company my dad had worked for since the day he'd graduated from high school in 1951.

Wallace Edwards took what came without complaint. When he began at Milliken's Excelsior Finishing Plant in Pendleton, South Carolina, he hoisted hundred-pound rolls of cloth, but he slowly advanced up the company ladder until he reached a management position at Milliken's Robbins Mill in North Carolina. Along the way he spent much of his time training younger men who would get better-paying jobs than the one he had or would ever have. They had college degrees, and he did not. And although he tried to take the advancement courses his company offered, an erratic shift schedule made regular attendance almost impossible—as it did for so many who worked beside him. So he silently let that dream go, but even then I remember waking up early in the morning to find him in the living room, with his own mysterious pads and pencils in front of him as he watched what were to me bleak public television shows that taught the basics of probability and statistics.

Of course my father was not the only hard worker in the family. My mother made all her own clothes and most of my sister's too, and with fabric dad bought at discount from the mill she even fashioned sport coats for him and me. And she almost always held a full-time job too. Just after my sister Kathy and I got home from school, Grandma Pauline or Aunt Rita, mama's sister, would come by to watch us while mama went off for her 4:00-to-midnight shift at the bathing suit plant. But before she left she would always prepare our dinner—a real dinner—that we would always find waiting in the oven.

It wasn't often she could eat with us, but the meals she left behind were exactly the kind she prepared when she could sit down at the table with her husband and children. It might be pork chops, green beans cooked with ham hocks, crowder peas in their own thick juice, freshly cut creamed corn, and corn bread burned a little on the bottom for my dad. Or it might be my favorite, fried chicken, mashed potatoes, and always from scratch, biscuits. And everyone who knows my mother knows her pecan pie and her chocolate cake. There is still nothing in this world I'd rather eat than mama's chocolate cake.

In spite of the strain of their work, my parents always found time to take us on trips, and those I liked most were camping trips to Hartwell Lake—with Uncle Harold, Aunt Rita, and my cousin Tim. We would all pitch a tent and immediately take my uncle's bass boat out on the lake, with Uncle Harold or my dad steering while Tim and I skied double. We loved it, or at least Tim and I did, and as soon as we were up on our skis, the ritual would begin: Tim and I started catcalling each other every low and rude name that was permissible in the middle of July 1962 in the northern reaches of South Carolina. It wasn't long before we two would start to laugh and then just lose it and fall into the lake. My dad would sometimes look skyward, or slap his forehead, and then he and Uncle Harold would circle back to bring us the ski ropes, over and over, as he got more and more fed up with us. One time he was so worn-out with our apparently genetic inability to behave that, as we thrashed around in the water and choked on our laughter, he took off one of his shoes and threw it at us. We only calmed down when we saw the shoe bob and then, after floating innocently for just an instant, sink like a stone. For the rest of the weekend Wallace Reid Edwards stomped around, over rocks and through muddy ground, with one bare foot, while Tim and I moved about quietly, our faces as grave—well, almost as grave—as Bill Buckner's after he boggled that dribbling ground ball and lost the World Series for the Boston Red Sox—and for much of the universe—on that bleak October evening in 1986.

But if my parents were sometimes worn-out by us kids or exhausted by their labors at the mill, they seldom showed it. Below our house in Robbins, at the bottom of a slope, was a yard with a metal clothesline, an old swing set, and a plot of dirt at the end of which stood a tall four-by-four with a basketball hoop nailed to it. The former owner had called this overgrown, junglelike yard Monkeyland, and the name had stuck. I can't begin to count how many afternoons I spent shooting baskets there with my mother (who had been something of a star on her high school team). My friends often came over to shoot hoops, and if my mother came out to hang laundry while we were playing, she would shoot a little too. At those moments she seemed to be having the time of her life, and it always made me happy to see her doing layups way better than some of my friends.

It never occurred to me that anyone would have judged my world as being deprived of anything—or at least of anything important. It wasn't. In fact, back then, a world of greater privilege hardly even registered on my consciousness. It never really occurred to me that there was any other way of life. Beyond my Utica mill village I had seen that street of "superintendent houses," the big houses with fine lawns, but I am sure that I assumed that mothers inside those houses left nice pork chops warming in ovens before they headed out to work, and that the fathers sometimes threw shoes from bass boats at cousins treading water out on a lake. The houses were bigger and the clothes were nicer than mine. Beyond that, I saw no difference. In many ways, in the most important ways, I still do not. Of course, I now know that there are immense differences in what a person from a mill village and a person from the best block in town can expect from society—and often gets—especially at the worst of times.

Not until we moved to Robbins did I become friends with the first "wealthy" boy I was to know. His dad was the mayor of Robbins and his family owned Robbins's only department store. I remember going over to his house after we'd played a game of football. His shirt had gotten dirty, and when he went into his closet to get a clean replacement, he pulled out a brand-new shirt packaged in cellophane. I was amazed: it was as if the department store were his own personal closet. My mother made many of my clothes, and the idea of keeping a shirt in a closet all wrapped up in cellophane, with many other shirts just like it, simply amazed me.

Yet at that moment it amounted to only a curiosity. The

boy was my friend and that was what mattered. He was a gracious one too, and when he got older, I remember how happy he was to drive me around town in his first car. It seemed that only a few years later he became a minister. I liked the fine things his family had, but for the most part they surely didn't matter that much to him, and they didn't matter much to me.

Back then the ambitions I had were vague; I only wanted to please my parents. And they wanted me to do things that would make me happy. At first I didn't understand why they had such a strong ambition for me to find a life beyond a mill town. But at one of my early summer jobs in the weaving room of the Robbins mill, I began to understand how genuinely hard the life of my parents—and so many other people—really was. And why they wanted something different for me.

The weaving room was massive, with great throbbing looms and a big system of ducts that pulled as much dust as possible out of the generally foul air. The noise was deafening, the ducts poorly lit, and the lint that stuck to them was black and wet. I was sixteen, and my job was to clean those ducts. At night I would come home caked with sweat and covered with some obscure kind of residue, and my mother's face would always grow tense as she opened the door and I walked into her clean house.

The next summer I was older, and my job, which paid only a little more, was worse: clean the hundreds of looms fastened to the floor of the weaving room. They were slick with grease and lint, and because most of the loom fixers chewed tobacco to pass the time, they were also smeared with rank globs of thick, brown saliva. "Now you see," my dad said, bending close to me so that I could hear him over the din of the looms, "why you need to go to college."

During the canteen break I would sit with men and women in their lint-covered overalls, and they would talk to me about their sons and daughters—what they were like and the fine future they saw for them. I was struck by the dignity of these men and women. Like my father, they almost never expressed bitterness and they rarely complained. What was the point, perhaps, for they all knew they shared hard lives that were much the same. You saw that they looked out for each other and took care of each other, and that they were honest about things in general and about their lives. It touched me when the first millworker took me aside and told me I mustn't spend the rest of my life in a mill: "Son, you need to go to school." Many of them said the same thing to me when I worked at that mill. That's what they all called college—school—and of course I knew what they meant.

To help pay for that "school," first at Clemson and then at NC State, my mother came up with a plan to make just enough money for each fall semester. She would start her own refinishing business, for she was convinced that with work and imagination—and such demands never intimidated my mother—she could make a go of it. And she did—with some real success. For $15 a month she rented an old gas station on the highway and set up shop. Now all she needed was the raw materials, and perhaps someone to drag everything home behind her. So each weekend she kindly invited her college-age son to all the county auctions, where he saw nothing but sorry lumps of firewood where his mother saw fine heirlooms for a good front parlor.

My father's Christmas bonus just about covered the spring semester, but it left nothing extra for my parents, and I hated that. I was determined to ease their strain by finishing up in only three years, while working part-time unloading boxes for UPS and painting railroad crossings on state highways. I did manage to graduate in three years from NC State, where in the spring of 1974 I finished a textiles degree. That had been the dream of the mill-town boy who had started college only a few years before, but by 1974 I knew I wanted to be a lawyer, and in the fall I started law school at the University of North Carolina at Chapel Hill.

I might say now that law school was a big step for me, as were the even greater changes that would soon come. But none of that ever altered my relationship with my parents, or theirs with me—which is how it is with most people. Something small that happened in 1989 may give an idea of how, no matter what I was doing or am doing, I remained and remain the small-town son of Bobbie and Wallace Edwards. Although I had started practicing law in 1978, it took eleven years before both my parents managed to take off from work and drive to Beaufort to watch me on the last day of what was for me an important trial. I was representing an electrician who had been permanently disabled at a hazardous job site—and it was a complex and difficult case. On that last day it was a fine thing to spot my parents in the benches of the Carteret County courthouse. I remember my parents' pride that day. But I can't help remembering something else.

Just as I was marshaling all my reserves and calling to mind all the welter of necessary facts and figures and complications and long-range implications and all kinds of things I can't now begin to remember, and just I was poised to lurch into my closing arguments and begin my last impassioned appeal for justice, mama made a small gesture. She wanted to say something to me. My mind was already racing toward what I would begin to say to the jury, but I knew she wanted to wish me good luck, and I didn't want to deprive her of that. So I stopped, moved over close, and smiled down at her. She reached out and touched my arm. "Johnny," she said. "Johnny. Your necktie has a stain on it." I blinked, moved back to the center of the courtroom, and began to speak.

In law school, although most of my classmates were older than I was, age did not begin to define the real difference I perceived between most of them and me. These were not mill kids: they were the sons and daughters of urban professionals. They carried themselves with confidence, dressed well and spoke well, without any bashfulness. For the first time in my life, I felt out of place and I frankly wondered if I was up to the task.

My first class was civil procedure, where we were to learn the rules that govern the procedures in lawsuits. I sat all the way in the back pretending to be invisible. The professor began to call on students in alphabetical order. "Mr. Allen," he barked, and followed with a question that neither Mr. Allen—nor I—could answer. The professor tore into him. I measured the size of the class against the time on the clock and thought, *Please, God, let there be lots of A, B, C, and D names!*

"Miss Anania."

Miss Anania was seated several rows in front of me. She had the blackest hair and fine light blue eyes, and from the way she leaned forward and listened to the professor's question, it was obvious that she was deeply absorbed in the flow of his words and already amazingly aware—at least in my view—of every secret his question implied. Her answer was perfect. He asked another question. Another flawless reply.

And after another minute or two of this exchange, the

professor paused, then he turned to the class. "That's exactly right," he declared. "And what Miss Anania is doing is exactly what all of you should do. She understands the case in question, explores it with confidence." He then turned to the blackboard and began to diagram an analytical map of civil procedure that did not make the slightest sense to me, and only to me—of that I was sure. I sank further into my chair.

"Any questions before we move on?" the professor asked. Then, responding to the single hand in the air: "Yes, Miss Anania. Do you have something you wish to say?"

"Yes, I do" was the young woman's even reply. "That diagram's about as clear as mud. And if there's anybody in this classroom that understands it, I'd be absolutely flabbergasted."

The halls buzzed that afternoon with references to the Anania girl. I was at least as captivated as everyone else, although I took her performance as further evidence that I was way out of my league in the Carolina School of Law. At that time even the mildest suggestion that three years later I might get out of law school alive, and with Elizabeth Anania as my wife, would have seemed an absurdity.

But that's exactly what happened. On its face the notion that Elizabeth and I would become a couple was particularly implausible. She seemed to be everything that I was not. As the daughter of a Navy pilot who had flown missions over North Korea and China, Elizabeth had lived in Japan, Washington, and Florida. Not only was she well traveled, she was well read and had studied literature in graduate school before making the switch to law. And in the summer before she started law school, she had visited her parents, who were then stationed in Italy. I thought she carried herself as someone who had taken full measure of the world and had no doubts about her place in it. And without in any way appearing domineering, Elizabeth commanded her classmates' attention—while I struggled to prove to myself that I just belonged among them. I might also add that she was beautiful with those almost translucent blue eyes.

Fully a semester passed before I got the nerve to ask her out. On that first date, I took her to hear a band at the Holiday Inn just outside Chapel Hill. The music was too loud to allow much talk, and my dancing was only slightly better than middling, but she agreed to see me again. When she was sick and bedridden, I brought her a dove-shaped planter and some grape hyacinths. She let me be myself rather than compete with her sophistication. As different as our backgrounds were, at the core—our values, our aspirations, our determination— we were not different at all. She changed my world and my worldview and challenged my thoughts and most of my assumptions—and even my taste in food, which was somewhat hard. She still challenges me in everything I do. I soon came to understand that she had become my conscience, and she remains my conscience to this day.

On July 30, 1977, the Saturday after we took the North Carolina State Bar exam, Elizabeth and I got married in a small country church in Chapel Hill. The church had no air-conditioning, and the heat, as some people eventually admitted, was unreal. Elizabeth showed up with a 7-Up in her hand, and I had the $11 wedding ring that I placed on her finger as she placed a $22 ring on mine. We were married. We drove off for Williamsburg, Virginia, in my old Volkswagen, to the hotel and the dinner that had been prepaid by Elizabeth's parents. While we had a one-night honeymoon and toured candle-making shops and watched battle reenactments on the green, Elizabeth's parents, Liz and Vince Anania, did the hard work of packing our belongings and loading them into a rented trailer and hauling it to Virginia Beach. The next day they helped us move into the townhouse we had just rented. But that first night we would all meet at a Virginia Beach motel where we had reserved a room for them and one for us.

Elizabeth and I had no credit cards, and we discovered that between us we could not manage the $22 in cash for the motel room. We could only scrape up $20, and that included change we found on the floor of the car. The clerk at the hotel was sympathetic, but there was a strict policy and he couldn't let us into the room without full payment in advance. So for several hours during the second evening of our marriage, we sat on a burgundy Naugahyde sofa under the flickering fluorescent lights of the Lodge Motel and waited for Captain and Mrs. Anania to arrive and front us an extra $2. I have always wondered what they said, or even thought, about their new son-in-law on that night. I have never asked.

When Elizabeth and I married, our wedding vows spoke of our desire to raise a family. Two years later we had Wade and he became the center of our lives. At eighteen months, my son was always there at the YMCA youth basketball games I coached. We hauled our babies with us to restaurants, to movie theaters, to the mall. As Wade and our second child, our daughter Cate, got older, more of our social life revolved around their activities and interests. I coached both of them in soccer and basketball, took them to UNC basketball games, hosted their friends for sleepovers, attended Cate's ballet and drama events, belonged to the Indian Guides with Wade, and happily enough, was part of an Indian Princesses tribe with

Cate. Using the frequent flyer miles I had accumulated while taking depositions during the preceding years, we flew to Europe with them when Wade was eight and Cate was five. Wade had been taking Latin from a retired Latin teacher at Root Elementary who had volunteered to teach some of children the language she loved. Wade went to Rome with a list of places he had to see: the Colosseum, of course, and the Forum, and the catacombs. But more often our family trips were to see Elizabeth's parents or my parents in Robbins, where Cate would stand on a chair beside the drainboard and help mama knead the biscuit dough while Wade and I would shoot baskets in Monkeyland.

Since becoming parents, Elizabeth and I have vacationed without our kids only once—a three-day trip to Charleston when Wade was thirteen months old. I say that without an ounce of regret. Every good time we've had has been made better for our children's presence.

As demanding as my trial work was, it gave way to parenting. More than one judge heard me request that we adjourn early so that I could make it over to the soccer fields to coach a practice. But of course my kids knew how important my clients were to me. At weekly family meetings, I would recite my deposition and trial schedules while, from the age of seven through her eleventh birthday, Cate played secretary and faithfully recorded every commitment in our family journal. On the weekend before a trial, it became an Edwards family tradition to dine together at O'Charley's in Raleigh. Wade would order fajitas, Cate spaghetti, Elizabeth chicken, and I the fish. We'd talk about the case at hand, since it was always obvious that I couldn't concentrate on anything else. And during weekend recesses, I would shuffle downstairs to the kitchen on Saturday mornings and fix the kids pancakes shaped like animals—my expression of gratitude for their patience while their dad was in Trial Mode.

Between activities with the kids and the fact that Elizabeth and I were both practicing law, we seldom had time left over for purely adult socializing. I never felt shortchanged. Every December in Raleigh, we would throw a big Christmas party that allowed us to catch up with our friends, and to see them with their kids as well. Fifty or sixty children of varying ages would be upstairs with cookies and punch—and a baby-sitter or two we had hired to keep the peace—while their parents were downstairs eating the mounds of food Elizabeth had made in the weeks before. Everyone marveled at our collection of Christmas trees, particularly the one that the children always decorated themselves with cartoon characters and colorful socks and old mittens.

Washington has not changed my party habits much. As a U.S. senator, one of the benefits of my refusing to take contributions from Washington lobbyists or political action committees is that I don't feel I have to go to cocktail parties unless I really want to go, especially when I would rather be home with my kids. The focus of my social life has not changed, although I do have a new round of young children—Emma Claire and Jack—to decorate the children's tree.

Because we did everything as a family, our children became extremely close to us, and to each other. Unless there was a conflict in their schedules, Wade and Cate attended each other's soccer games and even each other's soccer practices. When Cate started kindergarten, her third-grade brother—with no prodding from us—would wait for her class to finish, then walk her home down the path next to the creek, holding her hand the whole way. Although I did my best to be a good big brother to my sister Kathy and my brother Blake, I take a backseat to Wade in this department. Once, when the children were about ten and twelve, a Raleigh neighbor went crazy and began firing a gun outside his house. Wade calmly took Cate into a walk-in closet in our bedroom and sat with his frightened little sister until the police restored order.

It's no coincidence that as my personal life became increasingly filled with family activities, I gravitated toward cases involving good folks like the Campbells whose families had been tested by tragedy, but who still clung together even as they reached out for help. I don't care how corny it sounds: it was nothing short of an honor to fight for ordinary people who in times of crisis exhibited such love for each other and such extraordinary strength.

I am grateful that my home was one where decency was the daily bread. But of course that had been the only world I had known. I was caught flat-footed for a time in law school when, awed by the poise and polish of some of my more privileged friends, I feared that in that world decency was an insufficient currency. I was wrong. What worked in the mills of Robbins worked in the halls of the law school, and in county courtrooms, as it does in Senate chambers. There are few things I know better than this: the right to dignity—at every level of society—is and must be one of the chief guarantees of a civilized society.

• • •

At a time when the lives of my son and my daughter had become the center of my own life, the saga of the Howards—

among the finest people I will ever have the privilege of serving—was one I took especially personally. I still do.

What I wanted to be as a father, Greg Howard already was.

In a lawsuit revolving around Greg's tragic death, I told the
jury that he was no Superman. But, in fact, in some ways he
was better than Superman, for the thirty-year-old North Car-
olinian worked to save souls as well as lives. Greg was a Methodist minister, an emergency medical technician, a volunteer
fireman, and a member of a rural rescue squad. While earning
his biology degree at Methodist College in Fayetteville, he led
a campaign to save dozens of trees from a campus clear-cutting
project. A dedicated naturalist, he considered the land and the
human body sacred trusts from God. He lectured on campus
for ecological awareness and against student drinking. He
sang in the college choir and drove its bus. As a young minister, Greg logged hundreds of miles throughout eastern North
Carolina to pray with the sick and the dying. And in the
summer of 1987, he fulfilled his dream of directing an outdoor ministry at the Elk Shoals United Methodist Camp in
the foothills of northwestern North Carolina. At the three-
hundred-acre retreat, Greg taught hundreds of children their
responsibilities as God's stewards of the earth, working eighty
hours a week in the service of his deeply held beliefs. An avid
canoeist and cyclist with a mountain-man beard and a lively
sense of humor, he could start a campfire or take apart a trac-
tor as capably as he could quote Scripture. By the age of thirty,
Greg Howard was already a man in full.

Yet his greatest talent was as a father. From Joshua Allen
Howard's infancy, it was obvious that he was infatuated with
his daddy. Greg's wife, Jane, was more than happy to cede the
bathing and diaper-changing chores to her husband, and it

amused her along with everyone else to see the little boy wearing precisely the same camp attire as Greg, right down to the matching keychains on their belt loops. The boy shadowed his father everywhere—on the campground, at the fire department, on ski slopes—and everything that Greg did prompted a stream of questions from the boy: How does this engine work? What does that wire go to? Greg supplied the answers, which his son soaked up and then regurgitated to astonished strangers. At the age of three, Josh was carrying a miniature tool kit, taking apart machines and waxing cars with his dad. He protested to his mom that he never wanted to go to school: his daddy could teach him everything worth knowing.

Nonetheless, Josh came to like preschool at the day care center. On the morning of February 29, 1988, his dad dropped him off at 8 A.M. and told the boy that he'd pick him up at three that afternoon, like always. The boy did not know that his mother was pregnant, and that Greg and Jane were driving to Winston-Salem that day to shop for maternity clothes. And of course, he knew nothing at all about a textile company in Troy, Michigan, called Collins & Aikman or that one of its drivers was at that moment barreling toward the northwestern North Carolina town of Yadkinville in a thirty-thousand-pound tractor-trailer. The driver, who could by law work no longer than a twelve-hour shift, was paid by how many miles he covered in those twelve hours.

At 5:30 that afternoon, the teacher at the day care center phoned its owner to say that Josh's parents had still not picked him up. The owner left a note for Greg and Jane on the door of the center, then she took Josh home to her place. "When are my mommy and daddy coming?" he asked. He would not eat dinner. It was getting close to bedtime when the owner phoned the sheriff's office, but it took three calls before they would give her any information. Then she told Josh that his parents had been in an accident, and he started to cry. His father had presided at many funerals, and the parsonage where they had lived before coming to the camp abutted a large cemetery.

"They're dead, aren't they?" Josh finally said. But the woman did not feel it was her place to break the news to him.

Then the boy said, "The dogs at the camp haven't been fed"—the several stray dogs Greg had taken in during the past year. So the owner's husband went out and bought some dog food, and they drove Josh out to Elk Shoals, where Josh showed them how he and his father had always fed the dogs. Then they drove the boy back to their house, bathed him, and put him to bed. The following afternoon, a relative finally arrived to tell Josh Howard what he must already have known. His whole world, as his grandmother Golda Howard would testify, "just fell into little pieces."

• • •

But Golda Howard put the boy's world back together.

Although a bastion of strength and goodness, Greg Howard had nothing on his mother. An Army nurse and elementary-school teacher, Golda LaWon Sloan Howard had already been dealt a world of suffering before the deaths of her son and daughter-in-law. Her eldest son had been killed in a freak car accident when he was twenty-one. Six months later, her husband, an Army colonel, died as well, as did her brother soon after that. Then she was diagnosed with breast cancer less than a year after attending her brother's funeral. When at the age of sixty-six she responded to Greg's death by declaring that she would raise her four-year-old grandson, a number of relatives reacted with disapproval. Despite the boy's obvious attachment to her, they simply could not picture a senior citizen filling such a huge void in Josh Howard's life all by herself.

As it turns out, they did not know this woman. Perfectly at ease with kids from her teaching days, and well seasoned by life's tragedies, Golda Howard matched her grandson's energy as few adults half her age could have done. She enrolled him in swimming lessons and art classes, signed him up for soccer and basketball, went camping with him and pitched their tent. Twice they drove cross-country to visit her only surviving son, Touché (so nicknamed by his father to indicate his certainty that the son would "make his mark on the world"). As Golda steered, Josh would study the map, recite state capital names, and select motels. What the grandmother did not know about car engines or the outdoors, the grandson had already learned. And a half dozen times every year, Touché put his own career on hold to fly from Idaho to North Carolina and be the big brother to Josh that Greg had always been to him.

Despite his modest minister's salary, Greg Howard had taken advantage of every investment opportunity the Methodist church offered so that his son might be provided for. With what Greg had put aside, along with church stipends and her own retirement funds, Golda would manage to see to all her grandson's needs. She had never needed much for herself. To this day, Golda Howard drives the same car she drove when I met her in 1989, and she lives in the same unassuming one-story brick house in Fayetteville, a few miles south of Fort Bragg.

• • •

Like Greg Howard, Golda did not shy away from a fight, and here was an important fight. She felt tremendous grief over the loss of her son, but she felt tremendous outrage too. Greg and Jane had been mauled when a tractor-trailer driver had been encouraged by his company to stay behind the wheel too long, and—to make good time—to take many risks along the way. That stretch of Highway 421 was only two lanes, a strip studded with private driveways and broken by intersections. After over twenty-seven years with Collins & Aikman, the driver knew the dangers of that road well—and he knew too that his empty tractor-trailer would take much longer to stop than a truck carrying a full load. But he also knew that the more miles he covered in the allotted twelve-hour day, the more money he would be paid. So he was moving fast.

As the trucker headed east on Highway 421, two cars were ahead of him on a long, flat straightaway. The man in the first car had begun to slow down and had on his right turn signal to turn into one of the driveways up ahead. The second car was not slowing down as quickly as the signaling car in front of him. The truck driver moved up on the two cars. Both cars and the truck were moving along when the first driver stopped for a third car that was starting to come out of the driveway he was preparing to turn into. To pass him, the car behind the first car suddenly darted to the left and continued on his way. The truck driver was already almost on top of the signaling car when he slammed on his brakes. His tractor-trailer began to skid, then a moment later, it jackknifed into the westbound lane—where it crawled over the top of Greg and Jane Howard's oncoming Honda Civic.

And in a moment, a four-year-old boy lost his parents.

Collins & Aikman's insurance carrier's response to this

tragedy was all too familiar. The agent came to Golda Howard's door and offered a cash payment if she would sign a document waiving her right to file a claim against Collins & Aikman. She sent him away.

When the truck driver pleaded guilty to the charge of reckless driving, as Golda Howard had insisted, the Yadkin County Superior Court Judge did a most unusual thing. After ratifying the plea agreement and sentencing the driver to three years of probation and community service, he said from the bench, "I feel compelled to comment that I would hope that the grandparents of this child would have a consuming concern with doing what is necessary to provide for the future of this child. . . . There is the opportunity there arising out of this guilty plea and the circumstances of this case for the child at least not to have to worry for the rest of its life about financial concerns. . . . I would say from the bench that I hope you folks will seek legal advice about the civil side of this lawsuit, and not attempt to settle it on your own with the insurance carrier."

Jane Howard's parents did not heed the judge's advice: they settled with Collins & Aikman for a minor sum. As a result, Josh's mother's death could not be introduced in any civil action. Greg Howard's mother, however, did not intend to let the textile company off so easily. She asked her son Touché Howard to contact his old Fayetteville High School classmate Mark Holt. Wasn't Mark out of law school now? And who could he recommend to handle a case pitting a sixty-six-year-old grandmother and a four-year-old boy against a half-billion-dollar corporation?

Mark said he worked with a guy at Tharrington Smith who might well be interested.

• • •

A good lawyer can never stop learning. Up until the time I left the courtroom for the chamber of the U.S. Senate, I was constantly trying out new questions during jury selection, or new ways of presenting exhibits, or a new order in which to introduce my witnesses. By the time I tried the Howard case in 1990, I had been chief of the Raleigh firm's civil litigation division for eight years. Both my caseload and my responsibilities had significantly increased since Wade Smith had deposited E.G. Sawyer's file on my desk, and so at any given time I was handling two or three dozen cases through varying stages of development—some still being researched to determine their merit, others in discovery, some in settlement negotiations, still others approaching trial.

Although I juggled the caseload and often learned something in one case that helped me in another, a few weeks before a case came to trial, I quit juggling, and that single case became the focus of my complete attention. I'd spend anywhere from ten to twenty hours each day absorbing the deposition transcripts, poring over medical charts and reference materials, calling up lawyer friends and bouncing ideas off them, and in all kinds of other ways cramming myself full of facts and theories. Only then could I walk into the courtroom with a coherent theory of the case and a flexible outline for proving it.

It's a system that can work only if you trust your associates and know how to benefit from their strengths and skills. Remembering how quickly the partners at Dearborn & Ewing in Nashville had ushered me into the litigation combat zone, I never hesitated to entrust younger lawyers with crucial tasks. Lawyers—like football players—can learn only so much on the sidelines as they watch the first team grind it out. It's ultimately to the client's benefit that the whole legal team be fully engaged and fully utilized in his case, and anyway, fairness requires it. A younger associate who does research, contacts experts, lines up depositions, and assembles exhibits should not be left scribbling on legal pads and sitting there mutely throughout a trial.

When he brought the Howard case to Tharrington Smith, Mark Holt was new to the firm. I had never worked with him, and I knew him only as an awfully likable minister's son with a choirboy's face. By the time I left my legal career for the U.S. Senate in 1998, Mark had tried more cases with me than any other attorney. He was smart and dedicated, he felt a genuine empathy for our clients, and he rose to every challenge I handed him.

I remember when I assigned Mark his first deposition of a medical expert. "You'll be there too, won't you?" he asked nervously. I assured him that I would, and I did appear—about three hours into the deposition, just as I had planned. When I finally did show up, Mark knew from the smile on my face that he'd just been initiated. And I knew from his smile that he'd done fine. I had confidence that Mark had the makings of an outstanding lawyer. In the Howard case he showed that he was already an excellent one.

•   •   •

Golda Howard was anything but vindictive. She believed that the truck driver who had killed her son had made a careless mistake with tragic consequences. The driver seemed like a decent man, and she believed his remorse was genuine. She had no interest in stripping him of his livelihood, imprisoning him, or in any other way compounding the terrible events of February 29, 1988. A great tragedy had come into her life and into Josh's, but she in no way wanted the truck driver's family to be devastated as hers had been.

The truck driver's employers were something else again. Golda was unswerving in her belief that unless the textile company became an example, other such businesses would continue to tacitly encourage their drivers to engage in reckless conduct. And that encouragement would cause other children to lose their parents and perhaps even their own lives. In one of our depositions, a Collins & Aikman official made the flip remark that in the transportation industry, it was "a given that some lives would be lost." Golda was livid when she heard what he had said.

It was Mark Holt who discovered the legal basis that allowed us to pursue a claim for punitive damages. The precedent was *Marsh v. Trotman,* a 1989 state appellate case in which a young girl in an automobile had been badly injured by a collision with a tractor-trailer. The court had ruled that it was the truck driver's "willful or wanton operation of a motor vehicle," rather than some mechanical defect or sudden distraction, that had led to the injury—and that such reckless conduct made punitive damages allowable. Since, at Golda Howard's insistence, the Collins & Aikman driver had pleaded guilty to reckless driving, we believed that the *Marsh* standard applied. I delegated the responsibility of arguing this pretrial motion to Mark.

My decision to entrust so important a matter to a relatively inexperienced lawyer unsettled our co-counsel, Billy Richardson. Billy had been hired by the Howards because they saw the value of retaining an attorney from Fayetteville, where the lawsuit would be tried. A bright and engaging young man who would later serve two terms in the North Carolina state legislature, Billy was as sure an asset to the Howards' cause as was Mark. It was a good team because we each had different strengths. And the case would best be served if we divided responsibilities according to those strengths, so Mark would handle the legal research and depositions, Billy the local court matters along with the investigation of the accident scene near Yadkinville, and I would handle the examinations and arguments in the trial itself.

This division of labor played a huge role in the outcome of the Howard case. On the strength of Mark's brief, the defense's pretrial motion to dismiss our punitive damages case was denied. The judge who ruled in our favor, Cumberland County Superior Court Judge B. Craig Ellis, had been Billy's choice to preside over our case. Ellis had been the judge in a murder trial Billy had recently handled but I was concerned that he hadn't heard any big civil cases and might be inclined to throw out a substantial jury award, just as the judge had done in the Campbell case. But Billy insisted that Ellis would be fair, and he was pleased when the case was assigned to him.

A gabby fellow not unlike my friend David Kirby, Billy also proved to be the right guy to canvass the accident scene. At the local Amoco station near Yadkinville, he struck up a conversation with the man behind the counter—who, it turned out, knew several of the eyewitnesses. In chatting up the first state trooper who had arrived at the accident site on Highway 421, Billy learned that the Highway Patrol had tapes of several interviews with the witnesses. Billy Richardson gathered the names of potential witnesses, then Mark Holt deposed them.

Meanwhile, I directed our trial strategy—and I found that the Howard case was hitting closer to home than I had anticipated.

• • •

Now seven, Greg Howard's boy had keen, searching eyes and a relentlessly inquisitive mind. Unlike his father, his chief fascination was history, not science, and he seemed to care more about his grandfather's military career than his dad's commitment to the Methodist church. But like his father, the boy was good at anything he put his mind to, and I continued to see evidence of that long after the lawsuit was closed. Fifteen years after the loss of his parents, Josh Howard graduated in the top ten of his high school class and received an award for involvement in more activities than any other student in his school. His father would have been proud.

I was no Greg Howard, and my son Wade was quite different from Josh. But I knew all about the intimacy of their father-son bond, for Wade also went everywhere with me. By the time of the Howard trial, Wade was nearly eleven—already a fine writer, a nut for the UNC Tar Heels basketball team, and forever asking me questions about the cases I was working on. He was far and away the most fastidious Edwards in the household, and the first among us to master a computer. Wade had a calmness that I sometimes recalled as people talked about their dear friend Greg Howard. It was something more than the levelheadedness I had—there was a bit of a preacher's composure in my son. If his friends sprayed the fire extinguisher all over the wooden floors in the kitchen while we were out to dinner—which they did—he would calmly tell us not to worry about it, he'd clean it up, and he would start mopping. As much as I loved Wade, I spent a fair amount of my time just being amazed by him.

But above all, I spent time *with* him. And not a minute of it, no matter what we did or didn't do, was anything but precious. "Father and son" didn't quite describe it, for Wade and I were best friends. Although Josh was young when Greg died, I had no doubt that they too would have become best friends.

There came a time when I sat in a hotel room in Fayetteville as I prepared for the trial and began to think about how to talk to the jury about damages. I decided to list the various things that Josh would miss. His father would not be there to teach Josh how to throw a curveball. Or how to drive a car. Or how to get over the first heartbreak. Or how to select a college. Or how to be a good husband. Or how to be a good father.

The list, I soon realized, was hopelessly inadequate. The treasure in a father-son relationship was more than what you got, it was what you shared. And I thought of what Wade and I had shared. Soccer victories. Watching the Tar Heels play basketball. Trips to the beach. Trips to anywhere—the post office, the store for milk, whatever, wherever—just going places together, or just him in my arms on the couch, as we told each other stupid jokes or said nothing, absolutely nothing. That fierce, clumsy, inarticulate loving speech of the heart, exhilarating and reliable—Josh Howard would miss all that.

•   •   •

It must be said that trials such as these, even at the end, are hardly festive events. They involve, above all, the intricate and often graphic retelling of a tragedy. Some clients are so befogged by the recollection of the experience that it's difficult to get them to focus on the legal issues at hand. Others become caught up in the apparent theater of it all. They see their lawsuit as a crusade, and when the gavel is banged for the last time, they're somewhat lost. One of my clients, a nice woman whose husband died of a disease that could have been arrested had the doctor's office not misfiled his chart, seemed completely at a loss after we'd won. "What next?" she asked me. It broke my heart. She knew the answer, of course: getting on with a life without her beloved husband. That was next. And there are clients who at trial discover their "inner lawyer" and cannot resist the impulse to bombard their attorneys with suggestions of the most dubious kind.

Josh Howard's grandmother was the perfect client. A short but sturdy Midwesterner who had lived on military bases from Alaska to Bolivia and had cared for the sick and sometimes severely injured, Golda had a reservoir of toughness that had helped her abide her long string of losses. She was at bottom a practical woman who believed in hiring the right people and then trusting them to do their work. When her opinion was called for, she never hesitated to give it, and during jury selection Golda sat beside me and frequently responded to my questions and offered her thoughts. Sometimes, however, she did speak up without being asked. One of the prospective jurors was a truck driver, a seemingly disastrous choice for us, but during *voir dire* the man seemed so receptive to our position that I momentarily flirted with the idea of letting him stay on the jury.

Then: "Get that guy out of here!" Golda Howard hissed into my ear, and I came to my senses.

We had asked Golda to write a history of Greg's life—

where he had worked, what organizations he had belonged to, who his friends were—and so in the months before trial, she wrote out just some of what she remembered about her son. To ensure that her grandson would not see her cry, she accomplished this sad task during the hours when Josh was at school. And on Wednesday, June 6, 1990, she sat stoically behind the plaintiff's table in the Cumberland County courthouse while emergency technicians, state troopers, and other eyewitnesses described the terrible end of her son's life. I never heard so much as a sigh from her.

The following day, Golda Howard took the stand. "I want you to tell the jury a little bit about what kind of boy Greg was when he was growing up," I said.

The compact, white-haired grandmother sat there for a moment. "What could a mother say about her son," she murmured. "He really was the kind of child other mothers wanted their children to play with. He was courteous and well behaved and thoughtful."

Greg's mother did not color her testimony with a multitude of adjectives. She simply listed his deeds, and that by itself took a long time. After Golda was done, I showed her a letter Greg had written to a doctor who had expressed concern about whether young AIDS patients should be allowed to attend the Methodist camp at Elk Shoals.

"Would you read to the jury the last two paragraphs of Greg's letter, please?" I asked.

She did: "The risk is in what the community and other campers and other parents think—a social problem rather than a medical problem, but also a theological one. You told me the first time I met you that you had never turned away a patient and that you had come here as a missionary physician. I am a missionary, also. It is my job to offer Jesus Christ to people in a variety of outdoor learning experiences. In the last fifteen years, I have not worked at a camp that has ever turned away a child who wanted to come. All I can think of, is that if we refuse admission to a program of ministry, then one day . . ."

Golda Howard began to cry. I took the letter from her. "That's okay," I said. I would read what followed in my closing argument:

". . . then one day we will have to answer the question asked in Matthew 25: 'Lord, when did we see you hungry, or thirsty, or a stranger, or naked or sick or in prison, and did not minister to you? Then he will say to them, Truly, I say to you, as you did it not to one of the least of these, you did it not to me.' I think you see my dilemma. Any suggestions would be most helpful. Sincerely, Greg Howard, director."

• • •

Compared to some others I've tried, the Howard trial was relatively brief and straightforward. But it didn't feel that way at the time, for throughout the presentation of our case, the air was heavy with grief. Witnesses cried; jurors cried; the court reporter cried. I had been talking to myself as much as to Mark Holt and Billy Richardson when I reminded them more than once, "We need to keep our emotions in check."

From the emergency technician: "His body was broken up. Bones were protruding from his body, his arms and legs. And I knew there was nothing, you know, we could do for him at that time."

From one Elk Shoals employee: "Joshua was like a little shadow. He went right behind Greg every footstep that he would go. . . . They were very close. They were in the process of building a tree house at the time of Greg's death."

From another: "He was such a gentleman. I remember one night in my cabin, there were four girls just bawling their eyes out because they were homesick. Greg came out and just calmed all of them down. He told them stories until they went to sleep."

From another: "I saw him try to teach Josh how to skip a rock across a river. Josh would try, and his rock would go down. I saw him bend over him almost as if he had a golf club, as you see golfers training their children how to hit the ball. He was holding Josh's hand and showing him how to hold that rock to skip it across the river. That took patience, and he had a lot of that."

From a close friend: "When Josh lost his father, Josh lost a man with the capacity to be a friend—one of the greatest friends I've ever known. A man that knew how to care, a man who could feel Josh's pain, as I feel my son's pain, as every father does. He doesn't have that."

And finally, from Touché Howard, when Mark Holt asked him what he believed Josh lost when he lost Greg: "I'm the one that should be able to tell you that, because Greg took care of me as I was growing up. And the answer is I *can't* tell you that. I mean, I've thought about that a lot every day for the last two and a half years.

"I think that there is no way that we will ever understand everything that Josh lost when he lost his dad. What he really lost was the chance for every day to be a new adventure with

Greg. Because that's the way Greg lived his life. Every day was a new adventure. Josh was there with him, and he made it a new adventure for Josh."

None of this was gratuitous. Presenting the carnage caused by the Collins & Aikman driver was necessary to illustrate the magnitude of his recklessness. Greg's virtues and Josh's adulation of him were necessary to demonstrate the magnitude of the damages, which extended far beyond whatever Josh would no longer receive from his father's wages as a minister and camp director. Reducing loss to quantitative terms can feel like a crass exercise, but the law requires it.

The figures bandied about by either side amounted to only the barest measurement, much like the list I had compiled in my hotel room of what the absence of a father would mean to Josh over his lifetime. But the sheer irreplaceability of Greg Howard, I would argue, could not be used as a rationale for letting Collins & Aikman off the hook.

Josh was entitled to compensation for the economic loss that his father's death caused—his expected wages as a minister. No one argued about that. Yet people like Josh lose far more than a paycheck multiplied by months or even years. The law reflects mankind's deep regard for lost love and lost talk and support and guidance, for lost care in sickness, and the loss of advice on life and death, and sometimes even just some advice concerning how to best deal with the bad-tempered man in the house down the block. It was the onerous duty of the law—and twelve men and women—to value Josh's loss.

Under the North Carolina law that we cited in the case, a company was responsible for damages caused by its employee in the commission of his or her duties. The employee's negligence was *its* negligence. And, we argued, by financially encouraging the driver to rack up as many miles as possible in the shortest amount of time, the company in fact produced its employee's negligence.

I felt somewhat sorry for the defense attorney. This was a case he should have settled with us, but his hands were tied by Collins & Aikman's insurance carrier. He could muster no counterattack to the volumes of testimony extolling Greg Howard's worth as a man and as a father, and so for the most part, he wisely let our character witnesses leave the stand without cross-examination. When he did question our witnesses' testimony, he often came off looking petty—as when he implied that Golda Howard had supplied inaccurate information about her dead son's income.

Particularly ill-advised was his decision to bring to the witness stand an economist who testified that the figures we had projected for Greg's net worth were grossly inflated. In any case, our contention was that Greg's earning potential constituted only a tiny fraction of what Josh's loss would be. That the defense focused on this tiny fraction seemed petty and mean. Worse still, their witness was an academic with a law degree, a Ph.D. in economics, and a desire to ridicule the venerable Dr. J. Finley Lee, our economist. I'd used Dr. Lee in the Sawyer and the Campbell trials, as well as in so many others, because no one had more experience in handling the nearly impossible task of helping a jury—and for that matter, me—understand what terrible human loss can and must count for, in necessary economic terms. His numbers were unassailable—erring, if at all, in perhaps being conservative—and he projected the air of someone who knew what he was talking about, someone the jury could trust. I never had to prepare

Finley Lee for a deposition. I just sent him the file and then let the other side do what they could with him.

And I knew the economist hired by Collins & Aikman. I had coached his sons in soccer and I liked him. He might have thought I would give him some leeway because of that friendship, and though as a man and a friend he could count on me, as an economist and a witness, he had to stand or fall on the merit of his testimony.

"Are you familiar with Dr. Lee's qualifications, the person you've been criticizing here today? Are you familiar with his qualifications?"

"Yes."

"Are you aware that he's had his Ph.D. for twenty-five years now?"

"Yes."

"Are you aware that over the years he's consulted almost on a yearly basis with various agencies of the United States government? Did you know that?"

"I did not."

"Are you aware that he's consulted with, I think, thirty-eight of the fifty state governments in the United States?"

"I was not."

"Are you aware that over the years he has continuously consulted with private businesses both in North Carolina and *outside of North Carolina?*"

"I was unaware of that."

"As I recall from your deposition, the last time you have held a job in the private sector, a permanent job, was when you were twenty-one years old; isn't that right?"

"No, that's not right."

In fact I established that this expert had been a cabdriver

when he was twenty-one. But he pointed out that he did now consult in the private sector—for his wife's market-research firm. "I do not hold myself out as a consultant for every business that comes along," he sputtered.

"Well, you don't consult for *any* businesses except the businesses that are involved in your wife's business, do you?"

"I've been—I've consulted for forty law firms in connection with litigation."

"You've consulted in lawsuits?"

"That's right."

"Like this lawsuit?"

"That's right."

"You've talked about the various publications that you've had over the years. Tell the jury how many publications you've had dealing with the calculation of losses in personal injury cases."

"Zero."

This was just the start. Their expert had testified that we were wrong to assume that Greg Howard would have lived another forty-two years. In fact, the expert said that by applying a host of variables, he had determined that an American male had only a 50 percent likelihood of living to be seventy-two. Dr. Lee's estimate of economic losses, the economist concluded, should be lopped in half. I overcame the temptation to grin when I heard that.

"You are a lawyer, are you not?" I asked. "And you're licensed to practice in North Carolina?"

"That's correct."

"In doing the calculations that you have presented to the jury today, did you take into account the law of the State of North Carolina?"

The expert became wary. The defense, he said, "did not consult me because of my legal services."

Was he not aware, then, of the state mortuary tables that, unless there was evidence that Greg Howard had health problems, *required* the jury to assume his life expectancy would be seventy-two years? In which case, "you have undervalued the damages, have you not?"

The man's self-assurance was gone. "If the law of North Carolina says I'm to disregard known probabilities of death," he conceded, "then I have undervalued the damages."

Finally, to underscore that their expert's calculations simply did not square with reality, I observed, "You also made a deduction for self-maintenance, the money that Greg Howard would have spent on himself, did you not?"

"That's correct."

"In making that calculation, did you make any effort to determine what, in fact, his habits were, what he did spend on himself during his lifetime?"

"The answer is no."

"You also indicated in calculating the value of loss of services that you assume that half of his services would have gone to his wife, and half to Joshua?"

"That's right."

"Are you aware that his wife is dead?"

Gulp.

• • •

Cross-examining the driver was far trickier. Fearing it would prejudice the jurors' opinions, Judge Ellis had ruled that we could not introduce the truck driver's various other traffic violations, including a citation for tailgating just months after Greg and Jane Howard had been killed. And we could not introduce into evidence that Collins & Aikman had eventually fired the driver. Instead I was left to question an openly remorseful churchgoing man who, as his wife had testified, had stood before his congregation and asked them to pray for the Howard family. And though he no longer drove for Collins & Aikman, he remained its appealingly human face—a folksy counterweight to the friends and family of the man he had killed.

But the driver surprised us. Despite his testimony in his guilty plea, despite his deposition, despite everything that was known about the events of February 29, 1988, he now, for the first time ever, claimed that he had done nothing wrong.

The Collins & Aikman lawyer asked him, "Did you drive that truck carelessly and recklessly and in wanton disregard of the rights and safety of others as you drove down that roadway?"

"No, I did not," he replied. He had merely pleaded to that charge—the very charge, of course, that laid the basis for our claim of punitive damages against his former employers—"on the advice of my attorney at the time."

That the driver might suddenly change his tune was something we hadn't anticipated. No doubt he felt obligated, for whatever reason, to help out his former longtime employer. Whatever his motive for changing his testimony, his credibility was now in question, so I took my time as I changed the direction of the cross-examination.

First I laid the groundwork on recklessness.

"You can't stop a tractor-trailer as quickly as you can a car, can you?"

"Not quite as quick."

"The day that this accident happened, at the time it happened, your tractor-trailer was empty, wasn't it?"

"Yes, sir, it was."

"And you knew that a tractor-trailer that was empty was more difficult to stop than a tractor-trailer that was loaded, didn't you?"

"Yes, sir."

He acknowledged that he was responsible for establishing an adequate braking distance and for keeping his vehicle under control. He agreed that Highway 421 was a dangerous road. And he admitted that the distance between him and the car in front of him had been "between three and four truck lengths." Between 165 and 220 feet.

"Do you know how long it takes to get a tractor-trailer stopped that is going the speed you were going that day, fifty-five miles an hour?" I asked.

"About three hundred feet," he said.

So by his own calculations he had failed to maintain an adequate distance. And in skidding he had failed to maintain control and had slid across the double yellow line into Greg Howard's lane. In essence the driver admitted to all the facts that formed the basis of the guilty plea that he had just disavowed.

"Before you pleaded guilty," I said, "do you remember being put under oath the same way you were put under oath before you testified here today?"

"Yeah."

"And you swore to tell the truth, did you not?"

"Yes." But, he added, "The lawyer told me what to say—

I mean how to say it, and the judge asked me if I understood it and all of that."

"So you said something in the courtroom under oath that you believe not to be true?"

"On the advice of my lawyer, I pleaded to the charges that they put up there."

And so had he been telling the truth to the judge?

"As a result of the plea bargain, I guess not."

But, I reminded him, that judge had already listened to some of the same witnesses who had testified in this courtroom; and he had indicated his satisfaction, based on their testimony, that the driver was indeed guilty. Did he remember that?

"No," the driver said sullenly. "I don't know what he done."

• • •

Still, I spent the weekend in Raleigh fretting over his testimony. Whatever the driver had or hadn't pleaded to previously, he was sticking to one aspect of his story—namely that the little car in front of him had darted around the stopped vehicle before he could see that it was there. That Saturday evening I ate with my family at O'Charley's in observance of the family tradition. Everyone ordered their usual fare: the fajitas, the spaghetti, the chicken. And the fish for me. As we ate, I brought up the driver's claim that he couldn't see the stopped vehicle until the car between them had pulled around it.

Elizabeth dropped her fork. "Are you kidding?" she said. "He was driving so high up he should've been able to see for a half mile. Haven't you ever been in one of those trucks before?"

I didn't know that Elizabeth had. But as I've said before, she was a great deal more worldly than this Robbins boy.

I excused myself and called Billy Richardson in Fayetteville. "Get a truck up to the scene of the accident and take some photos."

Sunday morning Billy and Touché Howard drove up to Yadkinville and found a truck driver who loaned them his tractor-trailer in exchange for $200. While Touché drove, Billy shot a roll of film from the cab of the truck. When they got back to Fayetteville late that evening, Billy called a friend who operated a photo lab. They stayed up developing and printing enlarged photographs until three in the morning. Just as Elizabeth had said, the photographs showed that the trucker could clearly see beyond the car directly in front of him. At 9 A.M. on Monday we strolled into court prepared to introduce the prints as rebuttal evidence.

Instead Judge Ellis made rebuttal unnecessary. He agreed with us that we had conclusively established recklessness on the part of Collins & Aikman, so he directed the jury to find in favor of the plaintiff on the matter of negligence. All that remained was for the jurors to determine what if any damages should be awarded to Golda Howard on behalf of her grandson Josh.

"We could have played on your sympathies by having Josh sit here throughout the testimony," I said in my closing argument. But, I added, it would have been a cheap stunt, not to mention a traumatizing one, to force a seven-year-old boy to relive his trauma for the sake of a few tears. "Some of you may have noticed, though, when Dr. Finley Lee was testifying, a little boy came in with one of his relatives and sat in the back. He was there for just a few minutes, and then he left for good.

"That was Joshua Howard. This is his trial, after all. And his grandmother believes it's important that Josh be able to say someday, 'I attended a trial in the memory of my father. And, yes, I've lost him forever. But thanks to the jury I saw in court that day—thanks to the message they sent the trucking industry—maybe some other little boy won't.' "

•   •   •

While the jury deliberated, the defense attorney approached us. "Make us an offer," he said. Despite his best effort to seem relaxed, I could hear the worry in his voice.

I took the matter to Golda Howard. "Those guys know they've lost," she said. "Let's wait for the jury."

When the jury spoke, it spoke for Greg and Josh and Golda—loudly. But the moment after the award was announced, the sixty-eight-year-old grandmother seemed to have put it behind her. It was a good award—one that for many reasons, Golda does not talk about today. Golda always said it was never about the money, and as I have said, her life has not changed. She thanked her three attorneys, drove home to her grandson, and promptly flew off with him to Nebraska . . . to attend a family reunion.

•   •   •

There are two endings to the Howard saga—one quite happy, the other less so.

The trucking industry did indeed take notice of the verdict

against Collins & Aikman. As Billy Richardson would learn while trying over two dozen such cases in the wake of the Howard trial, trucking firms in the state of North Carolina were soon placing greater emphasis on driver safety training, and they were equipping more and more of their vehicles with governors to regulate driving speed. Some companies even abandoned the practice of paying drivers by the mile.

Unfortunately the insurance company also did what many powerful businesses do, and when the Republican Party took control of the state legislature in 1995, its lobbyists seized the moment. Soon a bill was passed disallowing punitive damage awards against a company as a result of an employee's actions, unless that particular action was specifically ratified by corporate officers. Meaning, among other things, that today Golda Howard would not be able to seek punitive damages from Collins & Aikman. Yes, our lawsuit had sent a message, and that message ultimately was: if you don't like the law, change it. Which, regrettably, they did.

The message to me, on the other hand, was one I'd confronted over my legal career and I'd grown to appreciate: if you can't help enough people being a lawyer, consider being a lawmaker.

• • •

Two years into my first term as U.S. senator, my office received an application in the mail. A seventeen-year-old North Carolina boy would be accepted at the United States Military Academy, if I, his elected representative, would give him a congressional appointment.

I've made a lot of tough decisions in the U.S. Senate. This

was not one of them. Josh Howard is now beginning his third year at West Point. He wants to serve in the United States infantry, though his grandmother, now eighty, would naturally prefer that he try something safer—like being a judge advocate general. But then Golda Howard never told any of her boys what they could or couldn't do. She just raised them to be fine men and, as she said, left the rest to God.

VALERIE

━━━◆━━━

I HAVE ALWAYS BEEN AN OPTIMIST, but I was a different kind of
optimist before Maundy Thursday, April 4, 1996. That was
the day my son died and my world stopped turning.

In spite of disappointments that had been real to me, up
until that day I had always known that mine was a happy life.
And I admit that all along I had a secret sense that it would go
on like that forever. I loved all the parts of my life, especially
when they came together—as they did on those nights before a
trial, when we all sat over the same dinners in the same restaurant, often at the same table, and my son Wade and my daughter Cate and Elizabeth and I talked about what would happen
the next day. They were the finest times I have known. I don't
think they could have been much simpler, and as I now recall
those evenings, as noisy as they were, I remember them as
quiet moments when my family was perfect.

Those dinners were a test for me. As complicated as my
work could be, and as subtle as every case surely was, if there
had been anything I was doing that I would have wished to
hide from Wade and Cate, then I had done it wrong. They
asked questions and I answered them—and then, rather often,

Elizabeth corrected me. I remember once hearing that some mother somewhere told a son that he should never do anything that couldn't be put on the front page of the *New York Times*. In any case my test was more severe. I decided to do nothing that I wouldn't want Wade and Cate to know about and understand.

I don't believe I was ever too much of an optimist in my work. Even when we lost a case, I knew we had made a step, and that sometimes it had been an important step. I knew that someone would win a case like it soon, and then someone else would win another. I believed then, as I do now, in the remarkable vitality of this country—in its ability to keep what's good and cherish what's fine, but always to change, get better, grow stronger, and become more just. How could I not be an optimist, and how could I not be happy? My days were so often full of activity aimed at something I knew to be good. I was stubborn, for I thought that with enough work, study, imagination, honesty, and sure goodwill, you could make anything and everything better. Of course I learned that some things can never be made better. Some things can never become right again.

• • •

My outlook had never been sunnier than it was in 1995 and early 1996. Two years before, I had opened the doors to my own law firm with my old law school friend David Kirby. We had often talked about our hopes of starting a small practice that would focus on a very few catastrophic injury and product liability cases, and it was now becoming a reality.

David and I had found office space in an old bank—the old

vault became our law library, and it pleased me greatly that David and I could walk to our offices from our homes, though I can't say we did that often. My mother took Elizabeth to an antiques warehouse in South Carolina, one of mama's favorite sources when she'd had her shop. For my office they picked out a fine old double-sided desk that had been owned by a Lowcountry lawyer, and for the tiny waiting room they found a moonfaced grandfather clock. Although David and I were nearly forty, we felt like kids as we watched the workmen nail up the letters. Edwards & Kirby. We just had to grin.

But trying a case and running a business are two different things. Opening a new firm, hiring secretaries, paralegals, a nurse, a receptionist, and even another lawyer—Mark Holt, my colleague in the Howard case—costs money. We knew a couple of things for sure. We knew that we would have to cover substantial costs, even hundred of thousands of dollars—for filing fees, deposition costs, fees to expert witnesses, travel costs—and we wouldn't recover any of it until after a case was over. And then only if we won. And we knew how much it cost to investigate whether a potential client's claim was meritorious before we even took a case. And if we didn't take it, we'd never get a penny of those expenses back.

It wasn't that hard to watch every penny. I'd learned to do that at my family's kitchen table. Edwards & Kirby did well from the start, and by 1995 our business had doubled.

And 1996 was going to be our most remarkable year. I was handling a case for two-year-old Bailey Griffin, the daughter of a Monroe farmer and his wife. In September of 1994, an obstetrician had attached a vacuum extractor to Bailey's head during delivery and fractured the girl's skull, causing blood to leak into her brain. Like Jennifer Campbell, Bailey was born with cerebral palsy, but her injuries were even more profound than Jennifer's: she could not walk, eat, talk, or sit up, and she was nearly blind. After several years of intensive medical care, Bailey died in the summer of 2002. As with the Campbells', Bailey's case involved a respected physician who had opted for a vaginal delivery when a cesarean was the far wiser course of action.

I never tired of representing people like the Griffins. Bailey's mother, Ashea Griffin, was unfailingly cheerful in spite of the challenges she and her husband Chris faced in caring for their severely disabled daughter. It was always good to see them, and each day I walked into my office, I was grateful for the turns in my life that had led me to this energizing and deeply satisfying work.

Each day was made even more pleasurable when my son began to work in my office. In the fall of 1995, at the age of sixteen, Wade became the Edwards & Kirby afternoon runner, or office gofer. It wasn't glamorous work: he copied exhibits and ran documents to the courthouse for filing, but he always wore a white shirt and tie and made the most of it. During slow moments, Wade would tease one of the pretty office assistants or try to get a rise out of me. To this day, when I walk into that law office, I see him in his chair near the receptionist's desk, waiting for an assignment and looking up at me with a grin from behind a newspaper, his thick throw of hair just like my own.

The young man in him was taking shape. I knew it, his mother knew it. And I am sure he knew it too. I could see it happening as he talked with his coworkers in the office, and I could see it at our house among his friends. Wade was a loyal and generous friend. He was the permanent designated driver, the one who helped others with their studies, the one who shouldered the blame for someone else's "miscue"—like that day when as a prank one of his friends unscrewed the hinges on our refrigerator door and left it there, precarious but still in place, until Elizabeth started making supper. And his graciousness extended to those well outside his circle. More than once I would come home in the evening to find Wade, in plaid flannel shirt and khaki pants, his back to the USA Soccer Team poster on his bedroom wall as he talked with some boy with spiked blue hair. The boy had sought out Wade because no one else at school would give him the time of day. Wade was like that.

Although I worried about my clients and their cases, I worried most about my own children, and in the way of most fathers, I generally underestimated their toughness. When Wade tried out for the varsity soccer team, I feared that he wouldn't make the team and that he would be shattered. I was half-right: Wade didn't make varsity. But he didn't go to pieces at all. He handled the disappointment quietly, with his customary grace.

In the summer of 1995, Wade and I decided to climb Mount Kilimanjaro with two friends. Rich Leonard had been Judge Dupree's other law clerk during my clerkship almost two decades before, and he had stayed my close friend. His fine, pensive, open-faced son Matt, already a student at Yale, was a few years older than Wade—but they got along well. After the plan was set for the four of us to scale Africa's tallest mountain, Wade looked for a climbing program where he could get acclimated to the thin atmosphere we would find at 19,340 feet. He chose a Colorado Outward Bound expedition for fifteen-year-olds, where he would learn something about mountain climbing and spend a week trying to breathe above 14,000 feet—still a good mile lower than where we were heading. I, however, was too embroiled in trial work to clear the decks for any kind of training, and even too busy to get my gear. On the eve of our trip, I walked into a Raleigh wilderness equipment store to buy a pair of hiking boots. The clerks were horrified, and I mean horrified, when I told them I'd be flying out the next day to climb Kilimanjaro. "At least wear them on the flight to break them in," one of them told me.

Nineteen hours before we flew to Africa, Wade returned from Colorado with an Outward Bound commemorative pin in his pocket and severe blisters on his feet. He was still walking gingerly on the sides of his feet as we cleared customs in Tanzania. Our mountain guide, John Mtumbe, would dub him "the boy with sick feet." I frankly wasn't sure that Wade was going to make it. But Rich, whose feet were one size larger than Wade's, volunteered to switch hiking boots with my son—and so dear Rich began to climb that amazing mountain in shoes one full size too small. At the hotel the night before we began our adventure, we asked the clerk, who spoke only Swahili and pidgin English, to bring us a bowl—and here we made vigorous circular motions—so that my son could soak his feet—and we pointed to his feet. Instead, the clerk brought us a soccer ball. Wade laughed and declared himself fit enough for the climb.

We had seen giraffes on the roadside on our way from the airport to the hotel, and now, as we started our hike to the base of the mountain and began to move through the lush terrain of Kilimanjaro, we passed our first troop of jabbering monkeys—and they raised our spirits. Wade continued to walk gingerly that first day, but our porters led us to streams where Wade could soak his feet, and by the time we began our climb the next day, he was ready to wear his own hiking boots again. My son was fine, but I was another matter. When the porters set up camp the third evening at a striking site beside a mountain stream, I pointed to a raggedy, sheer rock cliff across the way and asked one of them, "What's that over there?"

"That's what we're climbing tomorrow," said the porter. "Right after breakfast. That's why they call it Breakfast Hill."

I have never liked heights. One of the reasons I had wanted to climb Kilimanjaro, and the year before had attacked Mount Rainier, was to conquer my fear. I did not like the looks of Breakfast Hill. I began to chide Rich for choosing the back route, which was not only far less populated than the traditional path—we saw only one other group of climbers during our five-day climb to the summit—but also far steeper. It was a better test, Rich said, and although I would not tell him so then, I had to agree.

Shortly after we passed the 15,000-foot mark, Rich turned to me and said, "My head is killing me." Mine was too. Rich responded well to the medication Elizabeth had packed for altitude sickness, but I did not, and I grew lethargic and was unable to eat. By the fifth night, as we briefly encamped before beginning the six-hour push to reach the summit by dawn, I was feeling as helpless as a child. When it was time to start the summit climb, my son woke me. "How're you doing, dad?" I could only mumble, but he helped me pull on my thermal shirt and said, "You can do it." He put my boots on my feet and tied them. He kept talking softly and comforting me until I was dressed. And then he helped me up.

The four of us stayed together for perhaps two hours. But when a harsh chill set in around midnight, and the two boys wanted to pick up the pace, I simply couldn't go on. Rich sat next to me on a rock and asked me quietly, "What do you want out of this trip?"

"For Wade to make it to the top," I said, and I know I said it weakly. And so we agreed: Rich would go on with Matt and Wade, while I would stay behind with one of the porters.

They made the summit just after dawn. There at a height of nearly 20,000 feet, at a place the Masai call Ngaje Ngai, the House of God, my son told Rich and Matt, "I never would have thought that I would have been able to do something so hard." After an hour of rest, the three began the fourteen-hour journey downhill. Just then, a battered sight came into view. It was me—numb toes, pounding headache, busted headlamp, and all. Rich joined me for the short ascent to the summit. But the boys were ravenous. Since we had run out of food, they left the two geezers in what, in most places on earth, would have been a cloud of dust.

It took months for two of my toes to regain their feeling. But that wasn't what mattered. That trip to Africa with my son is worth a book in itself. It was worth everything.

• • •

Life resumed its more normal rhythms. Wade and I spent the fall and winter casting about for the next summer's adventure. Wade had his eye on the desert, so he began marking up his Outward Bound catalog. Cate and Wade both played soccer, although I only coached Cate's team that fall since the boys on Wade's team had outgrown everything an old football player could teach them. We made good on an old promise to take the children to New York City, and we flew up in the blizzard that blanketed the East Coast in January 1996. While the girls took in *Beauty and the Beast* on Broadway, Wade and I splurged on scalper's tickets and watched the Knicks play the Kings from some of the best seats in Madison Square Garden.

And there were some surprises. One day in February, Wade went to answer the phone, and when he came back, he informed us, with embarrassment, that he had been chosen as one of ten national finalists in the Voice of America Essay Contest. The essay he had written, entitled "Fancy Clothes and Overalls," described his experience going with his parents when they cast their ballots on Election Day:

"There are faces of old people and young people, voices of native North Carolinians in southern drawls and voices of naturalized citizens with their foreign accents. There are people in fancy clothes and others dressed in overalls. Each has exactly the same one vote. Each has exactly the same say in the election. There is no place in America where equality means as much as in the voting booth. . . .

"Soon I will be voting. It is a responsibility and a right. It is also an exciting national experience. Voters have different backgrounds, dreams, and experiences, but that is the whole point of voting. Different voices are heard.

"As I get close to the time I can register and vote, it is exciting. I become one of the voices. I know I will vote in every election. I know that someday I will bring my son with me and introduce him to one of the great American experiences: voting."

We wanted to tell everyone. He didn't want us to tell anyone, which was typical of Wade. This was, after all, a boy who—as we learned after his death from his high school English teacher—had participated in a weeklong discussion of the Hemingway short story "The Snows of Kilimanjaro" without once mentioning that he himself had scaled that great mountain. He wanted no part of the limelight, even when it was due him.

A few weeks after the call from the Voice of America official, Elizabeth, Cate, and I traveled to Washington, D.C., on Wade Edwards's coattails. We shook hands with First Lady Hillary Clinton and visited the White House. Wade went to Capitol Hill and met Senator Jesse Helms, who took to Wade, as most everyone did, and called the Senate photographer to take pictures, including one with Wade as senator, sitting behind Senator Helms's desk. There is no adequate way I can express the pride I felt for my son. As it turned out, his spring was to get better. Wade was also racking up literary awards for a short story that had been inspired by his Outward Bound adventures. Its title was "Summits":

"We stretched out under the tarp. It was smaller than the one the whole group had been under, but we had more room because there were only two of us. Since I had not gotten much sleep the night before, I was ready for a good night's sleep, and I did sleep for a couple of hours. Well, the sky was not ready for a full night's sleep. It was ready for war. First the wind started to pick up the edges of the tarp. I reached out from the sleeping bag and pulled it down. The cold came down my arm and chilled my ribs. Another edge flapped up, and Mike grabbed it. We had slept like this before. It would be okay. Then came the rain, icy knives of rain that turned to hail. For four hours we huddled together, closer than we had ever been in the group tarp, each with one hand stretched out to hold the tarp (our only protection against the weather) above us. Finally, the rain turned softer, and wind blew past us, and as they did, the sun came over the mountains. We pulled ourselves out from the tarp, ready to damn the sky, but when we looked the sky had become the most amazing color of violet, and the snow across the valley reflected a paler violet, and it was too perfect, too beautiful, too calm to speak, much less curse."

My son was a lovely writer. But through no prompting on my part, the law intrigued him even more. He told friends that one day he hoped to establish himself in his own practice. Once that was accomplished, he said, he'd like to join his dad at Edwards & Kirby.

That was a ways away. But the prospect of practicing law with my son was worth waiting for and worth living for, even if he was still only a junior at Broughton High School and was just beginning to worry about whether his SAT scores would get him into UNC. Around then he may have started to worry more, but I was worrying less. While Wade was on his own sort of winning streak and was becoming a young man of distinction, his father grew less and less fearful for him and instead became more and more optimistic.

I could not see how such a thing could end.

• • •

We all planned to meet at the beach house on April 4, 1996. Elizabeth and Cate flew back late that afternoon from a trip up North, and I picked them up at the airport on my way back to Raleigh from Charlotte, where I had just taken a deposition. We would go home and pack, then head for the beach. Wade and three of his friends had gotten a head start. They were in two cars, heading down Interstate 40 East, bound for Figure Eight Island and the house we had bought on the quiet

Carolina coastline where the kids could have fun. No one loved the refuge more than Wade, and he had been anticipating his spring break for weeks. Traffic was brisk that day, but behind the wheel of his black Jeep Grand Cherokee, with his friend Tyler Highsmith in the passenger seat, Wade took care, as he always did.

I cannot tell you why such care was not enough that afternoon. I can only say that there are fierce crosswinds on certain stretches of that interstate, and one of them swept my boy off the road. Tyler walked away. Wade was dead.

We were home packing when the state trooper's car pulled into our driveway. Before we knew it, friends had begun to arrive. One of them was David Kirby, and that evening he drove Elizabeth, Cate, and me to the hospital in Kenansville, where my son lay on a medical examiner's gurney.

My son Wade remains as alive in my heart today as he was alive in my heart then. He is just as alive there now, every day, as he was alive when I watched him eat pancakes in the kitchen or study in his room or talk to Cate about a million things or just smile and run his hand through his hair. Nothing in my life has ever hit me and stripped everything away like my son's death. That moment, those days, belong to our family. But because it was and is the most important fact of my life, and because I understand that I am now a public figure, I will say a few things about our son and about our loss.

The funeral service took place four days after the accident. Friends of Wade's and four of my friends—among them Rich Leonard and David Kirby—stood before the congregation and gave wonderful testimonials. Cate paid brave and lovely tribute to her big brother, but Elizabeth and I could not find our own words. She read a poem. I read passages from Wade's journal.

Our house was filled with friends and family. Then it was not. For many weeks, we felt nothing in that house but Wade's absence, and I can remember little about that time except that Wade was gone.

Cate saved us or at least taught us to save ourselves. She pulled two chairs together as a makeshift bed and slept beside us every night. She asked me to keep coaching her soccer team. She made us gifts and made us dinner. The three of us held on to each other, with our daughter the vital center.

• • •

But we were not about to let go of our son, and it was that determination that brought us out from the paralysis of grief. Elizabeth and I formed the nonprofit Wade Edwards Foundation, and our first project was a computer learning center that would be freely available after school to students in Wade's high school. Gene Hafer, a friend whose daughter had gone to day care with Wade, suggested that we call it the WELL, the Wade Edwards Learning Lab, and we did. The wonderful sculptor and now our dear friend, Thomas Sayre, designed a 106-foot undulating, tiered bench in the shady picnic area at Broughton High School. Designed to suggest the cometlike arc of a short but bright life, the sculpture included at the "head of the comet" a wall ornamented with the molded handprints of Wade's friends. In front of the wall, on the floor of a small plaza, there was an inscription taken from a Latin exam Wade had written when he was fifteen:

"The modern hero is a person who does something everyone thinks they could do if they were a little stronger, a little faster, a little smarter, or a little more generous. Heroes in ancient times were the link between man and perfect beings, gods. Heroes in modern times are the link between man as he is and man as he could be."

The following months brought other tributes to Wade. Even today tributes to our son continue to come to Elizabeth and me, and they touch us deeply. One letter arrived almost two years after Wade's death, and we hold it as a special gift. Back when our son had been a fifth-grader, he got to know a girl who was bused to Root Elementary from an economically disadvantaged and predominantly African-American neighborhood. Alyse Tharpe had a hard time finding her place in a school where so many other girls dressed in smock dresses and wore ribbons in their hair, and she felt isolated. As Alyse would one day tell Elizabeth, she always ate her lunch alone until the afternoon Wade Edwards got up from his own crowded table, came over to her, introduced himself, and asked if he could sit with her. That day he taught her how to play table football, and although he beat her at a game he knew so well, she later returned the favor by teaching him an outdoor game where she easily beat him.

Although they had been friends in elementary school, their paths had grown apart, and Alyse did not learn about Wade's death until one spring evening when she was working in the computer lab that had been named for her friend. Until Elizabeth and she began to talk that night, Alyse had never really connected the young man's face in the picture on the lab wall with the boy's face she had known—or the name of the lab—

with her Wade. She liked looking at his smiling face in that picture, and she had looked at it many times, but she couldn't quite understand what drew her to it. Elizabeth told her what had happened, and suddenly, two years after her friend's death, Alyse made the connection and the girl began to grieve. A few days later Elizabeth and I received the following letter, a letter addressed to our son. Many tributes to our son have been eloquent. None has been more eloquent than the one Alyse Tharpe gave to Wade.

> *Dear Wade,*
>
> *I just found out it was you that the Lab was dedicated to. I'd like to say that I'm Impressed and you wouldn't believe how much the students are grateful for it. There are some kids that do come in and cut up but I guess that's just you given them the sillies. I hear you climb a mountain! I'm proud that you climb it but that could never be me. I'm not that brave.*
>
> *Listen, I just wanted to say something that I didn't get to say when we attended school together. You were my only real friend and the only one since then. I want to thank you for being there and taking up for me when everyone else didn't. For sitting with me at lunch when I thought I had to eat by myself and making sure every-day was a good one. Even though I acted up all the time I'm glad I had someone to make me be serious when I needed to. I might not have gotten out of there without you. I have so much to thank you for because you make me the person I am. In being there for others, not judging, doing my own thing, being able to establish trust*

for and from other people. Thank you will never be enough neither will this letter or this poem but I hope that my heart is sufficient and my soul a light.

I don't feel sorry for you or sad other than the fact that elementary was the last time I saw you. I am hurt because of that. But your in a very special place right now so enjoy it. Don't send down no teardrops of rain because you're lonely (joking, cry all you want). You know what you did that was really special? You understood me most of the time and when you didn't you tried. When other people didn't understand me or what I was saying, they call me name, but not you! You were that light I tried and continually try to follow, but your too bright. I wont give up though. I come to terms that it was you that pulled me to that picture in the lab everyday. I'm sorry it didn't click. When your mom hugged me, I so badly wanted to cry, but I held it in. I didn't want to make her upset. I still make paper hats, footballs, and boats you taught me how to make and I still remember the last score in the last football game we played. 37–17!! I never beat you, you were just too good! God bless your soul, I love You.

White Sand
My friend, the white sand on the beaches,
that gives us heaven on earth.
And the sun that shines brightly over,
tripping on the clouds and winds,
of obstacles, but never hurt.
A martyr in my mind and others,
forever my brother.

Sunny days are when you smiled,
and life awakens to your pretty blue eyes.
My brother, white sand on the beaches and the sun,
pure as diamonds and precious as gold,
the bestest friend I've ever known.
When I'm sad, I hope your there to hold my hand.
When I'm happy, I hope your there to hug my neck.
Because if it wasn't for you my life would be a total
    wreck.
And for you my companion, I love you for that.
Your in my heart, forever!

Alyse's letter was another window into what we all had lost, but beyond everything else it was *his* loss—*his* being cheated out of a life in a world he had viewed with such idealism. The shards of a broken promise were everywhere: all over our house, on the television and the radio, on the neighborhood streets where he and I had jogged, and in the office I no longer visited. This has not changed in the seven years since Wade died, and I don't ever expect it to change. I do not fight it; it is the undercurrent of my life.

• • •

For six months after Wade died, I did not return to my law office. David Kirby, bless him, put the entire practice on his shoulders, told me not to worry, and visited our house every evening. If I've given the impression that my friend is an inveterate talker, let me make clear that he is also a wonderful listener, and I thank him for that. He and a friend of Elizabeth's, Gwynn Winstead, who had lost her own son Drew two decades before, essentially put Elizabeth and me to bed every night. I could not have asked for more loyal friends or a better friend that David. But it was not for David's sake that I decided one day to return to the office.

It did not serve Wade's memory any more than it served Cate's life for me to stand still hoping for time to turn back. And in any event I had little choice—my family and my work were all that could keep me held together. For months Elizabeth and I had worked to fund and build and furnish and equip the Wade Edwards Learning Lab, and by October 1996, that work was done and the learning lab had opened. So one morning that month, I dressed for the office again. I wasn't sure how I would pick up where I had left off when I once again drove to 3201 Glenwood Avenue and then walked past the reception area where my son used to wait for his assignments for the day. I stepped into my office, and I turned on the lights.

I knew that a little girl needed my help. And I suppose I needed hers.

. . .

Just as the Edwards family will always remember April 4, 1996, June 24, 1993, was a day that changed the world for the Lakeys.

On that warm Thursday afternoon, David and Sandy Lakey, he a software engineer and she a word-processing specialist, drove up to the Medfield Area Recreational Club with their five-year-old daughter, Valerie. They had done so almost every day after work since the pool had opened Memorial Day weekend. After they set up chairs and put down towels, Sandy returned home to make sandwiches for a picnic dinner; she brought them back to her husband and their only child, then she went off again to get her hair done.

David talked to some friends near the lifeguard stand while Valerie and a boy named Brandon took turns on the diving board. They would jump—arms flailing—swim to the ladder, then repeat the routine. The adults at the pool's edge knew the two five-year-olds were good swimmers.

As was customary, at ten minutes before 7 P.M., the lifeguard blew his whistle for the kids to clear the pool so that the adults could swim laps. Valerie and Brandon swam to the shallow end, and as they climbed the wide pool steps, Valerie asked if she and Brandon could play in the wading pool, and Brandon's mother took them over there. Near the shallow end of the adult pool, nearer the splashing children, David and Brandon's mother continued their conversation with friends. They were talking about the showers at the pool club, and Brandon's mother was moving back and forth between the conversation and the gate to the wading pool.

Brandon's mother later testified about what happened.

"We were just standing there talking when I heard Valerie say—I heard her call, 'Help'—it wasn't very loud. It was just a little, you know, kind of 'Help.' And I looked over to the pool and saw her sitting in the middle of the baby pool with her legs, you know, Indian style.

"And I asked her—I said, 'Honey, is this a for-real help or are you all just playing?' Because sometimes they would play, you know, 'Help-help,' you know. And so she said, 'No, this is for real.'

"And I hollered at David. I said, you know, 'Valerie's— Valerie says, "Help." Valerie—Valerie needs help.' "

"And I went around this way and came into the pool. And when I got there, David was already in the pool. So I'm assuming he jumped the fence, I don't know. I didn't see him because I was running into the wading area, but I didn't jump the fence. I came around this way, and Allison was right behind me.

"Valerie said she was stuck and couldn't move. And so, we—we tried to get her—we tried to get her up off the drain or off—we didn't know—I didn't know she was stuck on the drain, but I tried to get her up.

"And she couldn't—we couldn't budge her. David put his arms like, you know, under her—her legs and her back and pulled, and she was stuck.

"And Allison and I were right behind her in the water. And we tried with our hands to get underneath her—her skin to—to push her up. Under her buttocks. And we couldn't do that."

Brandon's mother went on, "Allison—Allison's fairly strong. She's a good swimmer. She's got good upper-body strength. And she was trying. And she looked at me and she said, 'I can't do it. I can't—I can't do it.' "

And back to Valerie. "She started saying that her stomach was hurting a little bit. And then we—at some point, one of us hollered, and I don't even know who it was—'Call'—you know—'Call 911!' And I don't even know who it was. I just know somebody did.

"And I remember seeing Benny—some things seemed like they were in slow motion. I remember seeing Benny on the phone, because I could see the phone. I could see him on the phone talking and pointing to his watch and talking, and so I'm assuming that's when he called, but I don't know.

"And we were still trying to get her off. And, I mean there was a lot—we were—you know, David was hollering, 'Somebody, help! Help me get her off. We can't get her off. She's stuck.'

"And again, we we were still trying to break the suction and we just—we couldn't budge her.

"Somebody went down to the pump house to turn the pump off. I guess thinking that that would—you know, that would stop the suction and—and let her off. And—and I remember David hollering, 'Cut it off. Cut it off.'

"And apparently, then at some point the suction broke, because he had her in his arms he—he just—it—when she came off the drain, it kind of pushed him back, you know, the force of—of it.

"And that's when I saw there was—the water was really red with blood and there was tissue all around."

David later testified that "at that point, I must have just been hysterical, because I just picked her up and held her. I laid down next to the pool and I just held on to her, and I prayed until the ambulance got there. And I don't know how long it was. It seemed like an eternity."

And David talked to her. Over and over again, "Daddy loves you. Daddy loves you. Daddy loves you."

A lifeguard was running across the parking lot as Sandy Lakey drove up. A little girl was screaming, "Valerie got stuck in the drain, and there's a lot of blood!" Sandy dropped the towels in her hands and ran to the baby pool, where her daughter was covered in towels and lying on David Lakey's chest beside the water. Brandon's mother was crouched down directly behind David.

"What happened?" gasped Sandy. "Did she drown?"

"Sandy," said Brandon's mother in a quaking voice, "I'm holding her intestines in my hands."

A trauma surgeon on call at Wake Medical Center led the team of doctors who saved Valerie's life after a five-hour surgery that evening. But the furious suction of the pool drain had torn out 80 percent of her small intestine and 50 percent of her large intestine. The trauma surgeon, a veteran observer of gunshot maimings, highway carnage, and burn victims, would later describe Valerie Lakey's injury as the worst he had ever seen. So extreme was her loss that he had to surgically implant a G-tube and a Hickman catheter to sustain her life with intravenous nutrition, also known as total parenteral nutrition, or TPN.

But after fifteen days at Wake Medical Center, five-year-old Valerie's lifelong medical odyssey had only begun. A colostomy, tube feeds, nutrition evaluation at a clinic in Boston, a stoma revision, and it went on and on. She went to bed with tubes hooked up to her body and began every morning by throwing up. Her kindergarten teacher learned to help empty her colostomy bag, a messy experience necessary after every meal—which is why Valerie began to skip most meals. Sandy continued to pack her a lunch of Gatorade and crackers, so that her daughter could at least pretend to be eating with her classmates, but her real meals came through IV tubes while she slept. Since the IV catheter increased her chances of infection, every cold or fever required a visit to the doctor.

Sandy and David Lakey could not sleep at night because the colostomy bag had to be emptied at least twice in the middle of the night, and because pump alarms went off whenever the tubes became kinked or got clogged with air bubbles.

Because the insurance allotment for home-nursing assistance had run out, Sandy quit the word-processing job she had held for the past fifteen years to care for Valerie full-time. It was where she wanted, needed, to be anyway. The strain that the horrific medical merry-go-round placed on the Lakeys was incalculable. But none of it meant a thing compared to the anguish of seeing their daughter suffer. She would always suffer. And eventually, the TPN might destroy her liver and her life.

And why? Why did all of this happen? Because of a wading pool drain cover that slid away so easily that any child could have pushed it away. Many had.

• • •

Like the Campbells, David and Sandy Lakey had married straight out of high school and seemed in every way a team. A pretty brunette from a small town in Illinois, Sandy had a face that was just made for good-natured laughter, a kind of 1960 Shelley Fabares face that neither evil or tragedy is supposed to visit. David, the more lean and contemplative partner, was a native of Weaverville, just a couple of miles from where E.G. Sawyer had been raised.

I took an instant liking to David and Sandy Lakey. As we spoke that first day, I was struck with how deeply they cared about Valerie and each other, how articulate they both were, and how David—who used such measured words—believed it was his duty to make certain that those responsible for what happened to Valerie would provide his daughter with the care she needed and would need for years to come. Their devotion to their child was absolute. Like Peggy and Jeff Campbell, who cared for Jennifer without complaint or bitterness, Valerie's parents assumed the formidable task of managing her medical needs. If no jury would find for them, they were determined to carry on without help.

Yet there was no end in sight. Caring for Valerie would cost millions of dollars in expenses for upward of a dozen surgeries and an endless procession of specialists, and David and Sandy would lose any chance of a normal life. Valerie would never have that chance. And like Golda Howard in her battle with the trucking industry, the Lakeys sensed a greater evil than the injury to their family. In 1991, only two years before Valerie's accident, at a pool club in Durham barely thirty miles away, another girl had been eviscerated by a swimming pool drain. So the Lakeys responded to their own tragedy with a kind of civic ferocity. David began looking into the pool inspection process, and he discovered that the law governing such inspections had been significantly weakened just before Valerie's accident—after much lobbying by the swimming pool industry. Outraged, David teamed up with a state senator to draft legislation expressly banning children's pools that did not have a dual-drain system and would make impossible the immense single-drain suction that had entrapped Valerie. He insisted that the language of the law be retroactive, even if that meant a tougher legislative battle. Then he sent out personal letters to every state representative who sat on the committee that would review the bill, and he followed them up with phone calls and with personal meetings, and he made it clear what he knew and what, with his efforts, everyone would soon know: that burying this bill would put many children's lives at risk.

David was a low-key programmer who was no more trained to be a crusading lobbyist than Sandy was trained to be an around-the-clock caretaker for a child whose small body had been utterly ravaged. But they both did what needed to be done. And Senate Bill 1517, requiring dual drains in every children's pool in North Carolina, became law in July of 1994. It would not have happened without David's work. And Sandy did her work too. After months of her mother's nursing and constant care, Valerie Lakey was strong enough to return to school . . . and she did, with much excitement. In the year since the accident, all three Lakeys could lay claim to remarkable achievements. Wade might have been thinking of David and Sandy Lakey when he wrote, "Heroes in modern times are the link between man as he is and man as he could be."

Valerie waited in the reception area the first time the Lakeys visited our law office in the fall of 1993. She was noticeably underweight and intensely shy. Nonetheless, she was undeniably adorable, with a tiny, sweet voice and her mother's innocent face. As I spoke to her, Valerie would look down at her lap, her chestnut hair would cover her face, and she would answer my questions reluctantly but politely, in that little voice. When I found the right words, like "Your dad says you and he like rock-and-roll music," she would turn her face up and the smile would come—broad and open, as if untouched by all that had happened. The thought of this beautiful, smiling child screaming in a pool darkened with her own blood was a ferocious image that day, and every day since.

As a legal matter, Valerie's case juxtaposed questions of products liability law—David Kirby's specialty—with the medical damages that had long been my expertise. David Kirby and I rarely tried cases together, but this seemed an appropriate time for an exception. In 1994 and 1995, David began directing the early research and witness-gathering in Valerie's case, while I finished up with a number of medical cases we had been handling. Through the end of 1995, while I was in other trials, David took a series of depositions of witnesses. The only deposition I believe I sat in on in Valerie's case was her father's, on the afternoon of April 3, 1996. I went home that night, and since Elizabeth and Cate were gone, Wade and I ordered pizza and watched a movie on the life and death of NC State basketball coach Jim Valvano. Wade died the next day.

On the morning of April 5, David Lakey telephoned our office from his mother's home in western North Carolina. He was the very first client to call about my son, and I was told that his voice was strained with grief. Later the Lakeys sent flowers to our house. You remember these little kindnesses. But I sensed more than kind sympathy in their gestures, for the Lakeys understood our pain. Three years before in 1993, on a day that had first seemed as ordinary for them as the fourth of April had been for us, their own child had come within a hairbreadth of death. They had not forgotten what that felt like; and as Elizabeth, Cate, and I were engulfed in sorrow, David and Sandy Lakey reached out as kindred spirits.

So when I finally returned to the offices of Edwards & Kirby that October morning in 1996, there was no question about how I would be spending that day, and the days to come. I came back to fight for the Lakeys.

• • •

But it was not going to be an easy fight. In addition to the physical and emotional trauma suffered by their daughter, David and Sandy Lakey had to confront the staggering expense of Valerie's ongoing medical care. That had to be our primary concern. Beyond that, the Lakeys knew that other children had suffered injuries similar to Valerie's and that other children would suffer similar injuries, unless something was done that would stop a company from selling a product it knew was defective.

The legal concept of "joint and several liability" means that more than one party may be held responsible for a single injury if each party's negligence or reckless conduct contributed to the causes of the injury. Valerie's case was just the kind of case for which this legal doctrine was intended, for we believed that four parties had been negligent and contributed to the tragedy on June 24, 1993.

The first was the Medfield Area Recreational Club. David and Sandy Lakey did not relish suing a facility where they and their good friends were members—and where they still visited so that Valerie could continue to play with her friends at the pool. In fact, by 1996 Valerie had joined the swim team at Medfield, and though she was weaker than some of the other swimmers and was encumbered by a dressing over her feeding line, she got a team trophy at the end of the season. Despite their hesitancy and despite their warm friendship with the pool manager, David and Sandy knew that the club had failed to maintain a safe wading pool—there was no question about that. The board at Medfield did not contest this even for a moment: Medfield carried insurance for precisely this reason, and it readily settled.

The second party was Wake County, whose health department was responsible for supervising the safety of the area's pools. The county conducted safety inspections, but the lax manner in which the inspections were routinely performed prevented the county from discovering this kind of dangerous condition in the wading pool. In fact, when a county safety inspector had checked the Medfield wading pool just thirteen days before the accident, he had stuck a pole into the water to see if the drain cover was in place, but he had made no effort at all to see if the cover was secure. The first response of the county was to do the inspections that they should have done all along. Within a week of Valerie's accident, Wake County's inspectors reinspected and closed fifteen area pools after discovering improperly attached protective drain covers.

The county's second response was to claim immunity from liability to Valerie. It invoked the "public duty" doctrine, a defense that, in many instances, protects a government agency from legal claims and exempts it from liability even when the agency has been negligent. We persisted, and in the end the county decided it did not want to test the public duty doctrine with a case involving the severe injury of a five-year-old girl and the county's manifest negligence. County officials directed their attorneys to settle.

The third responsible party was the pump manufacturer, Hayward Pool Products, for their pump had created the powerful vacuum that had almost sucked the life out of Valerie Lakey. Five years before the accident, when Medfield had purchased a Max-Flo pump from Hayward to provide circulation to the wading pool, which had a single drain, Hayward already knew there was a hazard of entrapment in a single-drain pool—it knew that an obstruction, like the body of a little girl over a single-suctioned drain, would create an immense vacuum—and yet it provided no warnings about that fact to purchasers. Nor did the company install vacuum breakers or shutoff valves. As two engineers whom we enlisted would explain in their pretrial depositions, a pump without vacuum breakers and relief devices was unnecessarily and highly dangerous. Not long after these depositions were taken, Hayward also settled with the Lakeys.

Valerie's injuries were eminently preventable—and because those in a position to prevent them had been negligent, Valerie Lakey would have to undergo a lifetime of hardship. The three parties that settled did so because they accepted the role their conduct had played in the great harm done to Valerie. Only one party refused to acknowledge its responsibility.

That company was Sta-Rite Industries, the Wisconsin-based pool products manufacturer. In 1984, after having purchased Swimquip and its entire inventory, Sta-Rite began to sell a pool drain cover that Swimquip had first designed in the 1960s. Medfield had purchased a Sta-Rite drain cover and had used it in the children's wading pool. From the day in January of 1994 when we filed the complaint alleging that Sta-Rite's drain cover was defective and dangerous, to the conclusion of the trial almost three years later, the company's position remained the same: it had done nothing wrong, its drain cover was not responsible for Valerie's injuries. The sole blame, according to Sta-Rite, belonged to the Medfield club's volunteer pool operator who had neglected to secure the drain cover in the wading pool.

In the children's wading pool at Medfield, atop the single drain was Sta-Rite's "anti-vortex drain cover"—a Frisbee-shaped device with four plastic prongs underneath it and two screw holes. An altogether different drain cover sat in the main pool at Medfield; it had screw holes but no prongs and an embossed reminder to use the screws. The Medfield pool operator—an engineer and a palpably decent soul—had screwed down the drain cover in the main pool, but in the wading pool he had merely used the prongs to snap in place the drain cover. He did not screw the wading pool drain cover in place because he believed that the prongs held it securely. That's what the prongs were there for, surely. "I had no suggestion that screws were necessary in the wading pool," he testified in his deposition.

"But you had also had no suggestion that screws would not be necessary in the wading pool, had you?" countered Sta-Rite's defense attorney. The volunteer operator's glum reply— "That's correct"—became the basis for the Sta-Rite's defense. According to Sta-Rite, their product was safe, and any injury caused by the drain in this case was caused by the pool operator's failure to use the Sta-Rite product properly.

If Medfield was having problems using the Sta-Rite product properly, it was not alone. We knew about the 1991 Durham accident involving a Sta-Rite drain cover, and in pretrial depositions we learned about another incident: a decade before in Henderson, North Carolina, a five-year-old boy had been entrapped and eviscerated due to the drain cover made by Swimquip. That made three horrific accidents within a fifty-mile radius—all of them linked to drain covers manufactured and sold by Sta-Rite or its predecessor Swimquip.

Was Sta-Rite in the dark about these incidents and about the safety risks of its products? Hardly. We subpoenaed documents about the purchase of Swimquip and discovered that as early as 1984, Sta-Rite knew about the 1982 evisceration of the little boy in Henderson and about other suction-entrapment cases. Company documents also revealed that throughout the 1980s, Sta-Rite officials had discussed the need for warnings and safety decals for its products with the company's attorneys, who had already defended the company in several claims resulting from drain-related accidents. In 1985, as these discussions were ongoing, Sta-Rite retooled its production process to emboss its logo on the drain cover, but no embossed warning was added. In 1987, Sta-Rite did add embossed warnings that could not be misplaced or washed away and would assure that pool operators understood that the anti-vortex drain cover was unsafe without the screws. Some of their new product line was released with embossed warnings. But Sta-Rite continued to manufacture and sell some of the "Medfield" drain covers *without* the embossed warning. It was luck of the draw who got the warnings and who did not.

And Medfield Area Recreational Club, without knowing any better, bought a Sta-Rite anti-vortex drain cover that arrived without an embossed warning.

• • •

North Carolina's product liability statute was not crafted with the best interests of Valerie Lakey in mind, to put it mildly. It provided companies with many ways to avoid liability. For example, it protected a manufacturer from liability if its product had been altered or modified from its intended use. The language of the statute was loose, and in that language, Sta-Rite took shelter. Sta-Rite's argument was that its anti-vortex drain cover, regardless of its appearance, was meant to be screwed down, and that Medfield's failure to screw down the drain cover amounted to an alteration or modification of the product. Medfield was negligent according to Sta-Rite, and Sta-Rite simply was not.

At Edwards & Kirby, we sometimes staged mock trials in front of focus groups, for it's a generally reliable way to test out certain arguments and case theories. We would bring in a small group of people from the same area the jury would come from, and as we argued the case to them, we would determine where we needed more emphasis, where we needed to be clearer, and generally how we were doing as we presented the client's case. Not every piece of evidence in a case will seem important to a jury, so which evidence do they find compelling? Did they understand "anti-vortex" or did we need an expert engineer to explain it? Was a diagram more useful or a witness's testimony? How were Valerie's complicated medical treatments best explained? Was the evidence of the enormous cost of Valerie's lifelong care clear enough?

In 1996, David Kirby tried Valerie's case before four different focus groups. All four times the mock jury found against him. Now the object of such exercises isn't to win, but rather to prepare, experiment, and learn, but still: four times! On the issue of damages, the groups were consistently with David, for Valerie's injuries were serious and they understood that. And the mock jurors were inclined to side with the plaintiff on the issue of Sta-Rite's negligence in designing a defective product and failing to provide a warning about its hazards. The sticking point for the mock jurors, we learned, was "alteration and modification." And Sta-Rite insisted that the failure to use screws to fasten the drain cover was an alteration or modification.

This information helped us direct our discovery better. David started scouring Sta-Rite's literature, catalogs, and instructions for anything that might address the mock juries' concerns. While wading through the thousands of pages of Sta-Rite company documents, David found a catalog for the same model of anti-vortex cover the Medfield pool club had purchased. Sure enough, there was the illustration of the disk-shaped object with the two screw holes, but the accompanying instructions mentioned nothing about screws. The language from the catalog, which we would introduce at trial and which I would quote in my closing argument, seemed clear: "The anti-vortex plate shall fit frame securely and be held in frame by four peripheral snap segments." It stated that the four prongs directly underneath the cover were the means of attaching it and—since there was no reference to any screws—of attaching it securely.

David couldn't believe it. Was the failure to mention anything about screws a typographical error? It did not matter. The company's own printed instructions supported the Medfield pool operator's contention that he "had no suggestion that screws were necessary in the wading pool." And that became the basis for our argument that no alteration or modification had been made by Medfield.

• • •

In the E.G. Sawyer case and the Jennifer Campbell case, the defendants were not malevolent but were caring and competent doctors who worked in good hospitals and yet made grievous mistakes. They had erred in their judgment, but no one could despise them.

In the Howard case and in Valerie's case, however, I was motivated both by my clients' losses and by the defendants' indifference to those losses. Collins & Aikman, the company whose negligence resulted in the deaths of Greg and Jane Howard, deserved punishment for financially inducing reckless driving. The remark made by a Collins & Aikman official that lost lives are an inevitability in the trucking business was a deplorable show of callousness. But such complacency is not only callous, it is treacherous.

And there is no reason whatsoever why a second injury should ever have taken place because of a defective swimming pool drain cover: the first time such a tragic incident occurred should have been the last. I believe that any decent person would believe this.

But Sta-Rite did not. As evidence poured into its office over the years that its products were maiming innocent children, it denied and avoided and obfuscated and covered up. In short Sta-Rite took extraordinary steps *not* to do the right thing—at extraordinary cost to others. There was not a single day during the trial when I forgot that.

The lead attorney for Sta-Rite was Gary Parsons. He was a big man, over six feet, and broad, with thick hair and a jovial face, although he did not smile much. He reminded me of my brother Blake, if Blake were ever to wear a suit. Since he had graduated from law school with David and me, Gary had spent a lot of time in courtrooms. Although we were neighbors, I was not feeling collegial. As we had done with Hayward Pool Products, with Wake County, and with the Medfield club, we had attempted to settle with Sta-Rite. We asked Gary to find out what Sta-Rite would offer, and what they offered was insulting. David and I knew it, and the Lakeys agreed. So trial was set for mid-November.

In the weeks leading up to jury selection, I worked as hard as I have ever worked in my life, but of course I had so much help. David did tremendous work in the dozens of depositions he took, and Bill Bystrynski, one of our newer associates, lined up witnesses and helped prepare briefs. During my six months away from the office, we asked Andi Curcio, who had worked for us a year earlier, to take a leave from teaching law in Atlanta so that she might root through the volumes of Sta-Rite documents. And the assistance provided by Laurie Armstrong, a registered nurse and workhorse, was crucial. Laurie's mastery of the discovery in the case, the exhibits as well as her understanding of Sta-Rite's own esoteric language and of Sta-Rite's cast of obscure characters, was both remarkable and invaluable. It would be her job at the plaintiffs' table to react to certain testimony by lunging for the appropriate document so that we could verify or refute what had just been said.

Jury selection in the Lakey case took a full week, longer than most cases take to try in full. We were looking for an intelligent jury that could see beyond two empty screw holes and comprehend Sta-Rite's neglect of responsibility. And if intelligence had been all we were after, the jury pool we drew would have been made to order. But some potential jurors reacted with visceral distaste to the very notion of suing a pool drain manufacturer over a child's injury. Others opposed lawsuits, period. As we quickly ran through our allotment of peremptory strikes, Sandy and David Lakey sat beside me and tried to bite down on their emotions. But it's hard to sit there and listen to strangers say, "Lawsuits like these are what's wrong with America!" and then go home to your innocent daughter and her feeding tubes.

During the *voir dire*, I questioned a young married woman who had no children and who worked for a bank. She was deeply skeptical of our lawsuit's merits and didn't appear likely to change her mind. "I don't like her," I whispered to David. At least, I thought I'd whispered it. In the closed courtroom, my voice had carried. I felt her look before I turned to see it—and we had used up our peremptory challenges. Like the obstetrician's daughter who had sat on the jury in the Campbell case, the banker on the Lakey jury would worry me until the verdict.

But the other side had also passed a juror likely to be sympathetic to Valerie and her parents. For reasons none of us could fathom, the defense did not strike from the jury a woman whose boy had died; she was as receptive to our case from the beginning as the banker was resistant to it. In between those extremes, the group included two engineers, an IBM employee who got along well with the banker, a hospital worker, and one independent-minded woman who was simply impossible for us or for the other side to read. It was an eclectic bunch—which is good. And there were good minds and hearts there, and I felt they would give Valerie a fair hearing.

Before testimony began, we took the videotaped deposition of Sta-Rite's chief engineer. David had already deposed him back in August, with uneventful results. After his deposition, however, Sta-Rite had produced documents we had been requesting for months, and when we reviewed the late-produced documents, we discovered that the engineer's signature appeared on almost every relevant memo. Over Gary Parsons's objection, I flew to Wisconsin on Sunday, November 24, and deposed the engineer the next day.

A reserved man who wore glasses and a sweater, he was an engineer right out of central casting. An employee of Sta-Rite Industries for twenty-three years, he knew that we were redeposing him for a reason, and he was not especially eager to give us any ammunition. By this point, I had studied reams of Sta-Rite documents and publications, and I had read the transcript of David's earlier deposition, and therefore I pretty much knew what the engineer would be inclined to say. And he knew that I did. And though the setting was nondescript— an office, a couple of lawyers, a videographer, and the deponent—the atmosphere in the bare room was as charged and tense as a packed courtroom.

Since the 1950s, Sta-Rite had primarily been a pump manufacturer, and then in 1984 it bought out Swimquip's product line and added drain covers to its own line of pool products. At that point, it was the engineer's job to approve those covers for an end-of-the-year production under the Sta-Rite name.

And so I asked the engineer what effort he had made to determine if any injuries had resulted from the use or misuse of Sta-Rite's newly acquired product. "Personally? I didn't."

Had he had any conversations with anyone about prior injuries the drain covers may have caused? "Not that I recall."

Had he made any effort to determine whether a particular hazard existed with these products? "No, not that I recall."

Was he, as chief engineer for Sta-Rite, familiar with the concept of a hazard analysis? "Yes."

And he had not conducted one? "Correct."

So basically he just took the product as it was and approved it to be produced and sold? "Yes."

Then I shifted gears. In 1984, when he effectively rubber-stamped these products, had he been aware of the 1982 Henderson accident in which a five-year-old boy had been disemboweled while trapped against a Swimquip grate? For that matter, was he aware of the study that Swimquip had commissioned on the precise question of the suction entrapment? Was he aware of the study's conclusion that—unless deflected by a proper drain cover—the vacuum force created by a pool pump "could trap and drown a relatively strong, aware adult"? The engineer said that he was not aware of the study.

Would that information have been helpful to him? Yes, he acknowledged, it would have been. But when I asked if such information might have inspired him to evaluate the Swimquip product's design, the engineer skirted the question and instead maintained, "If the screws are in place, it's not a hazard."

Still, his begrudging admissions were substantial, for they showed that Sta-Rite had dumped a product on the market without considering its hazards. The engineer's videotaped deposition, which we would show to the jury, laid the groundwork underlying this case: Sta-Rite's corporate indifference.

• • •

From the first bang of the gavel to the moment of final verdict, not a seat was empty in the courtroom of Wake County Superior Court Judge Robert L. Farmer. Valerie's horrible accident, and her parents' subsequent campaign to improve the safety of neighborhood pools, had received enormous press attention well beyond the Raleigh area. Reporters with their stenographer's pads sat next to young lawyers who whispered to one another. Courthouse employees and Medfield pool friends introduced themselves to each other as they sat shoulder to shoulder. Clerks worked quietly at their desks at the front of the courtroom or talked to the courtroom marshal, who, as he talked, kept his eyes on the courtroom and never looked at the clerk. When paralegals shuffled in or out the doors at the back of the courtroom, for a moment there would be sounds of chatter from the busy hallway. There was, every day of trial, an energy that would not, could not, be muffled by courtroom decorum. But only two things preoccupied me during those weeks: what was going on in front of me, and what had gone on months before on a highway to the beach.

A week after Thanksgiving 1996, testimony began in Valerie Lakey's case, and it was a tough day. Many in the courtroom found it agonizing as witness after witness described what had happened to a screaming little girl in a wading pool on June 24, 1993. There were nervous lifeguards, a university professor who had been playing with her baby in the wading pool, and a family friend who had watched—and some of them could not make it through their own testimony. When the doctors explained how in five hours of emergency surgery, they had done all they could to put a dying child back together, my mind would race to Wade and I had to struggle to maintain my composure. "I'm all right," I whispered when David leaned over and asked me if I was okay. I had to be. We could not let the Lakeys down.

On Thursday, December 5, we played the videotaped deposition of Sta-Rite's chief engineer, which I had taken the week before. The jury listened as in answer after answer he exhibited a total lack of concern about the risks of the products Sta-Rite had put on the market. He didn't know, he didn't test, he didn't get any studies. By the time he said, "If the screws are in place, it is not a hazard," his indifference was apparent, his excuse hollow. We followed that videotape with the videotaped deposition taken four months earlier of another Sta-Rite official.

David had asked him a fairly straightforward question: "Would you agree that the manufacturer of a product has an obligation to inform all of the users of its products of all the dangers that are known that are associated with the use of their product?"

"I don't believe that." The reply was chilling.

Two of our experts testified Thursday afternoon and much of Friday. The first, experimental psychology professor Harry Snyder, testified about how human factors relate to product use. He said that in the case of the anti-vortex drain cover, a person using the product could easily be misled about what was required to attach that cover securely. That the cover had plastic tabs that would attach the cover (but not secure it) could mislead someone. That there were no embossed or affixed warnings that the product had to be screwed down could contribute to the misperception. In other words, someone using the Sta-Rite anti-vortex drain cover could easily believe that it was unnecessary to screw the cover down.

Our star expert witness was consulting engineer Charles R. Manning Jr. A gruff, bull-shouldered man with a crew cut, Manning displayed a gift for plain, if sometimes terse, language. After giving the jury a history of pool pumps and drains, he explained how, in the absence of a drain cover, the centrifugal vacuum created by a pool pump could entangle hair, trap feet, or create sufficient suction to pull the intestines right out of the human body. And, I asked, had he thought of a solution for the defective design in the anti-vortex cover that would avoid the misunderstanding Harry Snyder had described?

"I did," he growled. "It took me two seconds, and it costs two cents."

Manning elaborated: the same kinds of captured screws that had been used in aviation for forty years, and that held covers on underwater lights to prevent electrocution, could easily be applied to drain covers. The captured screws stayed in the holes even when unscrewed, and thus they reminded the operator of the need to affix them and tighten them in place. Each captured screw cost about a penny more than the ones used by Sta-Rite. Two cents, in other words, and Valerie Lakey would have been spared her agonies.

I could see that the jurors were responding well to Manning and were greatly impressed by him. At one point I asked him a question and he didn't immediately respond, but instead glared at the wall with an impenetrable expression.

"Uh, Mr. Manning, did you hear my question?" I ventured.

"I may be old, Mr. Edwards, but I'm not deaf." The jury roared, and I roared too.

Those familiar with a courtroom know that testimony isn't always so engaging. Indeed, a trial's most important moments often turn on the written rather than spoken word—and documentary evidence can strike the public, and the jury, as tedious. During jury selection in Valerie's case, we had made a motion to subpoena all Sta-Rite's documents relating to its prior suction-entrapment cases. Gary Parsons objected. He argued that we should not be able to subpoena documents during trial, and that Sta-Rite had already provided all the responsive documents anyway.

In a strict sense, Parsons may have been right. Discovery does not usually take place during trial. After a lawsuit is filed, but before it goes to trial, the parties to the lawsuit can engage in "discovery" of evidence in the possession of the other side or other witnesses. During discovery the parties use various means to get evidence: among other things, a party can ask written questions called interrogatories, or ask oral questions in a deposition, or request that documents be produced. The answers are supposed to be complete and prompt. (See what I mean about tedious?) We had asked Sta-Rite to produce any documents it had involving accidents with its drain covers, and Sta-Rite had provided us with exactly two evisceration cases. Now, we hadn't asked for documents pertaining to all suction-entrapment cases or for documents involving Sta-Rite's predecessor Swimquip . . . and so Sta-Rite hadn't volunteered those. We continued to ask if there was anything more than the two cases, and Sta-Rite insisted there really wasn't anything left to hand over—they had "nothing to produce."

Judge Farmer listened to both sides. Then he said, "Well, why don't you bring in what you've got, and I'll rule on them case by case."

But days passed and no documents. We were well into our testimony when I again brought up the matter with Judge Farmer. Back in the judge's chambers, he asked Gary Parsons where the documents were.

"Your Honor," he said, "they're on a truck from Wisconsin."

I don't think anyone took a breath for a second or two.

"On a truck! I thought you said you didn't have anything! And now you're telling me you had to bring them here on a *truck?*" I had rarely seen a judge so angry. "You bring them to this courtroom the *moment* they arrive!"

On Monday, December 9, a dozen banker's boxes were carted into Judge Farmer's chambers. The very sight of them piled up beside his desk made the judge livid once again.

Gary Parsons pulled out the first file and handed it to Judge Farmer. "Your Honor, we would object to handing over this particular document on the grounds that . . ." As Parsons talked on, the judge flipped through the file, first reading, then flipping the pages. He waited for Parsons to finish his objection.

Then: "Denied." And Judge Farmer handed me the file.

"And this document, Your Honor, we would object to . . ." The routine was repeated.

"Denied."

The files piled up. In the depositions, we had received a few dark hints that more Valerie Lakeys were out there. Laurie Armstrong and Bill Bystrynski spent the next few evenings culling through the boxes of files. Some documents weren't relevant to our case, but some were staggering. A New Mexico boy whose arm was trapped in a pool drain and had drowned. A South Dakota boy eviscerated. An eight-year-old Texas boy who had miraculously survived after being held underwater for ten minutes while several adults fought to wrench his arm free from the suction. A Fresno girl who had died when her hair was entrapped in a whirlpool drain. Other head and leg injuries. Allegations of brain damage. Seizures. Deaths.

At some level, Sta-Rite knew all of this. Now we did too. And soon the jury would know it.

The day after receiving the truckload of documents, we made a motion to amend our original complaint to conform to the new evidence. We asked the judge to permit us to add a claim for punitive damages, based on Sta-Rite's willful and wanton negligence. Parsons protested that it was too late to amend the claims, but Judge Farmer was not sympathetic. He granted our motion.

· · ·

Friday the thirteenth of December, our last morning of testimony, began when eight-year-old Valerie Lakey climbed onto the witness stand.

Letting Valerie appear in court had been a painful decision—for David and Sandy Lakey, but also for me. As in Jennifer Campbell's case, we had prepared a "day in the life" video of the little girl and her parents. Like Jeff and Peggy Campbell, David and Sandy were seen as tender parents and warm caregivers, whether they were monitoring their daughter's intravenous line, attending to her colostomy bag, or simply putting their child to bed. Yet Valerie's challenges were much different from those of Jennifer Campbell.

Jennifer's video had presented the obstacles that a young girl faced and overcame—almost every day. That she could work through such things—a new movement of her body or just a new word—was real success, and anyone who watched her video felt the force of that success. That a brain-damaged child had such small victories each day was heartbreaking but inspiring, and, yes, there was always the sense that tomorrow things might be better still.

Valerie's video was different. Her life was harder to show, and it was also harder to watch. Although she was a bright girl who often spoke cheerful words in her shy and winning way, her video did not present a day filled with anything like Jennifer's minor heroisms and tender smiles. Much of the pain in Valerie Lakey's life was something Jennifer would never have to know, and much of it the world would never guess.

Today Valerie is more beautiful than she was back then— and she was genuinely beautiful back then. I felt that anyone looking at Valerie might imagine that hers was an easy, happy life—in spite of everything. The video we introduced showed otherwise. The video showed what Valerie herself could never say: that to maintain her basic functions, Valerie had to be attached to an intravenous line from twelve to fourteen hours each day, during which time she had GI feed tubes thrust into her stomach through a permanent apparatus she called her "button." For more than half of each day, as she was nourished and medicated by various fluids from various lines, this active young girl could hardly move at all. The strong antibiotics she took made her feel sick and in time began to corrode her stomach lining. The video showed her parents applying silver nitrate to burn off granulation around her central line, for the skin around the central line site had to be kept very clean. They had been assured by the doctors that Valerie would feel no discomfort, but she screamed in pain every single time. For no more than thirty minutes the jury would enter Valerie's other world, then they could turn away. That world would be Valerie's for the rest of her life.

Yet for the other half of the day this girl was abundant with life, and she did love life. When I'd visited the Lakeys at their home on the Thursday evening before Valerie's court appearance, she couldn't stop chatting. We talked about the hospital, and her TPN, and also some of the procedures that were part of her daily regimen. She was pleased to instruct me. When her mom brought out the earrings she had bought for Valerie's day in court, Valerie couldn't wait to try on her full outfit and put on the earrings.

The next day, she sat in the witness chair with her shoes dangling several inches from the platform, and those earrings were gleaming.

Because she was a child, I had to show that she understood her surroundings.

"Do you know where we are, Valerie?" I asked.

Her voice was only a whisper, or maybe less than a whisper, "A courtroom."

"That's right. And do you know who this man is?"

"The judge."

"And do you know who these people are?"

She stared at the twelve men and women looking at her from behind the wooden railing.

"My jury."

Her jury melted.

"Valerie," I said, "would you like to talk about what happened the day of the accident?"

She sat there for a moment. Then, in a barely audible voice: "No."

I wasn't prepared for this response and I wasn't sure what to say next. "Okay, then. We don't have to. Let's talk about some of the things you like to do."

And so, with some coaxing, Valerie talked about drawing, and swimming, and the name of her two cats. Then the little girl left the courtroom with her mother and father.

I've always believed in the virtues of respectfulness. Jurors watch how you treat not just the witnesses and the other attorneys, but the bailiff, the clerk, and everyone else in sight. If you're ingratiating with the jury but rude to a paralegal, then you've given them reason to doubt your decency and then your credibility. A courtroom is not very much different from anyplace else: you never win points by being a bully. Now, I admit that it is easy to get caught up in the rush of the moment in a trial—I have done it myself, I regret to say—but that is no excuse at all.

It came time for the defense to introduce the Sta-Rite officials as emblems of the company's earnestness. I thought about
the documents I'd seen about other children who had been
injured or killed—not by earnestness but by the company's
disregard—and I admit I felt contempt for the coming protes-
tations of high moral rectitude from Sta-Rite. But I did not
want to do anything in my cross-examination that might jeop-
ardize my clients' case or shame my parents. I tried to keep my
voice low and I kept my language courteous, but, let me tell
you, sometimes it was hard.

To the company's customer service manager, a twenty-six-
year veteran who had just finished extolling Sta-Rite's rigorous safety consciousness, I asked, "Before June twenty-fourth,
1993, did you know that a child could be trapped on a swimming pool drain and either die or be severely injured?"

"No, sir."

"Did your safety-conscious company tell you that in 1984
a young man named Adam Leonard had almost drowned and
that your company had been sued because of one of your
products being involved in that drowning or near drowning?"

"No."

"Were you told that?"

"No, sir."

"Objection to this line, Your Honor," said Gary Parsons.

"Overruled," said Judge Farmer.

"Were you told that an eleven-year-old boy named Richard
Hernandez was injured on a swimming pool drain in 1982?
Did your safety-conscious company tell you that?"

"No, sir."

After listing a few more injured children and receiving the

same response, I asked, "Did you ever participate in any discussion about how to make these products—that is, the drain cover involved in this case—safer?"

"Me personally, no, sir."

"Did anybody ever ask your advice, as the person who was responsible for servicing this product day in and day out, whether you believed there was some way to make this product safer?"

"No, sir."

On direct examination, the customer service manager had characterized Sta-Rite as a family-owned business in Delavan, Wisconsin. I wasn't going to let him get away with suggesting that he worked for some humble mom-and-pop outfit. Were they family-owned anymore? No. Now listed on the New York Stock Exchange? Yes. And where were its manufacturing facilities outside of Wisconsin? He volunteered Oxnard, California.

Also in Germany, perhaps? "Yes."

"In Italy?"

"Yes."

"In Mexico?"

"Yes."

"In New Zealand?"

"That I don't know."

"In Russia?"

"Yes."

I asked him if the anti-vortex cover that had been sold back in 1987 came with an installation instruction sheet. The customer service manager said he felt certain that it had.

"Did you bring that with you? Do you have it?"

"No, I don't have it."

"Is there anybody up there at the company that's got them?"

"I'm sure we can come up with it. I'm sorry. I don't have that available to me right now."

"But if we left today, you got on the phone, you could call somebody up there and get them to send it to you?"

"Objection, Your Honor."

"Overruled."

"I could try."

"Okay. I want to ask you to do that. When we break for lunch today, would you call the home office and ask them—do you have fax machines up there?"

"Yes, sir, we have fax machines."

"Okay. Would you ask them to fax you whatever instruction sheet it is that you've just testified is being sent with the anti-vortex cover? Would you be willing to do that?"

"Objection, Your Honor."

"Overruled."

"I'll try, certainly."

No such fax arrived because no such instructions existed.

• • •

And then there was Sta-Rite's general counsel, a man who had spent over twenty years as a lawyer but some time less than that venerating the law. He was a poster boy for corporate indifference. It was his job to coordinate the details of the purchase of Swimquip's product line in 1984. He acknowledged that "it was [his] responsibility to find out what hazards existed in the product line [Sta-Rite was] acquiring from Swim-quip," including "what had happened in the past with any of [the] products."

I began to call the names of the injured children we had only recently learned about, one by one.

"What did you determine, as your responsibility as general counsel for Sta-Rite, had happened to Anthony Benavidez?"

"I don't know."

"Can you tell the jury whether you did an investigation?"

"At this point, no, I can't."

How about a child named Butler? "Did you investigate that accident?"

"I don't know."

Dowdy? Dunham? Gustavson?

"Again, I don't recall."

He was, however, familiar with a case of a young girl who was disemboweled in 1981 on a drain that had not been properly covered.

"So in 1984 when you acquired Swimquip, you learned that the hazard existed of a child being eviscerated in suction entrapment when a drain was not properly covered, correct?"

"Right."

"You knew that in '84?"

"Yes."

"Did you tell the engineer who was responsible for this product about this hazard that you were aware of?"

"No."

"What did you do to make sure . . . the engineer responsible for this product knew what had happened to [the child]?"

"I didn't do anything."

"And whose responsibility would it have been to make sure the engineers knew about this injury and this hazard?"

"It would have been my responsibility."

Well, if there was a hazard, certainly a safety-conscious company would have investigated how to make the product safer. So I asked.

"Did [Sta-Rite] do anything to evaluate the cover, see if anything could be done to make it safer in 1984 before you put it on the market?"

"Not that I am aware of."

Sta-Rite recognized that a hazard existed, but the man in charge did not inform the engineers responsible for the product, and the company did not evaluate the cover to see if the risk could be reduced. In the meantime, certainly Sta-Rite was warning its customers, right? So I asked what he "did in 1984 to warn about that hazard that you knew about."

"We didn't do anything in terms of warning."

And in 1985, when Sta-Rite was sued for pool injuries and there was an allegation that the company had failed to supply any warning of the hazard of suction entrapment, "did you start warning about it in 1985?"

"No."

And then another case in 1985. "And now you're being sued again, and again the allegation is Sta-Rite is failing to give adequate warning of the hazard. . . . Did you start warning then?"

"No."

And then a third case in 1985. "When you got served with that third case in 1985, did you start to warn about the suction entrapment?"

"No."

And that's how it went. Again in 1986, and no warnings. But in 1987, Sta-Rite decided to begin adding inserts in its drain cover packages that warned of the hazard of suction entrapment. So it seemed like a natural question to ask, "Do you believe as general counsel for Sta-Rite in 1987 that you had a responsibility to warn about that hazard?" He had known about the hazard, he had known about the risk. And Sta-Rite had finally decided to act. The answer seemed obvious.

But the lawyer would not concede the obvious: "I don't know that we had the responsibility to do that."

Sta-Rite's counsel could not concede that it had a responsibility because even after the 1987 decision to warn, Sta-Rite had continued to make and sell drain covers without warnings—including the one that Medfield had bought for its wading pool. If the counsel had conceded that it had a responsibility, it would have damaged Sta-Rite's defense. But his failure to concede also cost Sta-Rite—in credibility with the jury.

If the Sta-Rite counsel was going to mount an unbelievable defense, I was going to let him. So I continued.

"The decision to put . . . the permanent embossed warning [on the drain cover] was the right way to warn about this hazard, correct?"

"Yes."

"And you thought that was the right and appropriate way to do that because it would be right there on the product all the time, right?"

"Yes."

"And that was a decision that you all had made . . . sometime in the fall of 1986, correct?"

"Sometime in '86, right."

"Okay. Did you as the lawyer for the company tell them that it would be okay after you had already made that decision, that it would be okay to go ahead and make products without the warning?"

"Objection," interrupted Parsons.

"Overruled."

I restated the question anyway. "In other words, you made the decision you believed they were necessary. You believed the right way to do it was to put it in the cover. Did you tell them that it was appropriate to go ahead and make covers after that decision was made without the warnings in them?"

"I don't recall."

"Would you believe today that it is fair and appropriate for the company to make a decision that it needed a warning and then make a product without the warning?"

"Yes, sir. I believe that's absolutely appropriate." And I was absolutely confident that the jury did not agree with the lawyer for Sta-Rite.

But the real man of the hour was the Sta-Rite official with the unfortunate title of "product safety coordinator." He readily acknowledged that it would have been his responsibility to do a product-safety audit of the Swimquip drains before putting them on the market in 1984. Could he show us such an audit?

"There is none," he said.

Was a hazard analysis done?

"No, not to my knowledge."

So much for coordinating product safety. When I asked him if he was aware of the previous suction entrapment cases, the Sta-Rite official said that he was not. Par for the course, I figured. While I had one reaction to the testimony, Judge

Farmer had quite another. Judge Farmer's face had changed colors.

At the next break, the judge demanded to see the lawyers in his chambers. His desk was piled high with stacks of Sta-Rite documents that had been brought to Raleigh by truck in the early days of the trial. While the product safety coordinator was testifying that he had seen nothing and knew nothing about suction-entrapment cases, Judge Farmer was apparently thinking about those documents he had been reviewing. As we stood silently, he rifled through them. Finally Judge Farmer pulled out a couple of pages that we had never seen. Parsons broke the silence with a bellowing protest. Judge Farmer put one hand up to silence Gary, and with the other he handed the pages over to us and dryly advised us to use them as we saw fit.

Judge Farmer had handed us correspondence that had passed between the product safety coordinator and another company official. The correspondence provided clear evidence that when the company official had asked the safety coordinator about past entrapment injuries, he had gone beyond a mere request for details concerning what had happened. He had in fact asked what the coordinator was doing to redesign the product and recall the defective product. In other words, the product safety coordinator *had* been aware of prior entrapment cases. He had lied on the witness stand.

The company official's letter proved that the safety coordinator had perjured himself, but it was the safety coordinator's complaint to a Sta-Rite lawyer about the official's letter that was really repugnant. "What is wrong with this man?" the safety coordinator had complained to the company lawyer. "Tell him to shut up. I have no intentions of answering these questions. And doesn't he know this kind of thing should never be put in writing?"

In the middle of one afternoon late in the trial, Gary Parsons informed the judge that he had run out of the witnesses for the day and suggested that the jury have the rest of the afternoon off. Judge Farmer was not cutting Sta-Rite any slack.

"Bring up someone or rest your case," the judge said.

Parsons was not ready to rest the defense's case, so he looked at his list of Sta-Rite employees who had been assisting in the case. He called a Sta-Rite staff technical writer named Coolidge to the stand. We knew nothing whatsoever about him. Parsons led him through a slow and uneventful filibuster of a direct examination until the last mundane fact about technical writing had been drawn out of Mr. Coolidge, and Parsons turned the questioning over to me.

I whispered to David Kirby, "What do I ask him?"

"I don't know." My partner shrugged. "Maybe ask him if he ever wrote a warning for Sta-Rite."

"Why?"

"So he can say he didn't."

I rose to my feet. Since I didn't have any better ideas, I led off by asking Mr. Coolidge if he had ever been asked to write a warning for the anti-vortex cover.

"Yes."

I did a double take. "Did you say yes?"

"Yes," he casually repeated.

"What—what did you do with it?"

"I gave it to them." Mr. Coolidge indicated the defense table.

Audible to both us and the jurors, someone at the defense table said, "Shit!"

The amazing thing was that Mr. Coolidge seemed absolutely oblivious to the importance of his words. He cheerfully called out to the defense lawyers, "Don't you still have it?" He was met with silence, then still cheerfully, he said to me, "I've still got a copy in my briefcase in the back of the courtroom."

Was this really happening?

"Well, then," I managed, "could you step off of the witness stand and get it for us?"

The room went dead quiet as the mind-bogglingly innocent Mr. Coolidge stood up and walked to the back of the courtroom. He returned to the witness stand with his briefcase, rummaged through his papers—all in complete silence—withdrew a sheet, and with a smile, handed it to me.

I studied it for a moment. "Would you please read that to the jury?" I asked.

He did. The warning that Mr. Coolidge had written concerning the anti-vortex cover was almost identical to the warning our experts had said—had insisted—should have come with the product. But that warning had not come with many of the pool drain covers sold by Sta-Rite—and it had not come with the drain cover that had sat at the bottom of the Medfield children's wading pool.

• • •

Not every day was so successful, and December 20, in fact, was quite rough.

Sta-Rite employed two expert witnesses to testify that their product was sound, but the first soon put his credibility in doubt by declaring—in spite of the testimony of all the other witnesses—that no warnings of any kind were necessary for the drain cover. Although his opinion isolated him from every other witness on either side, he became so indignant when I suggested that his testimony was damaging the defendant's case that he began a blustering and aimless monologue. When he finally ran out of words, there was nothing left for me to say but "Thank you for being here."

But the second expert, Dr. William Rowley, was different. He was in fact an extremely effective defense witness. A former major general in the Air Force and a consulting engineer who had designed swimming pools for the Olympics, Dr. Rowley had authored the 1974 Swimquip study that concluded drain suction "could trap and drown a relatively strong, aware adult." On direct examination he now said that *after* he had given his findings to Swimquip, the company's work had convinced him their product was safe. It was a pretty vague claim, but his short, clear answers were effective and strong.

When I asked him questions on cross-examination, however, he was no longer succinct, but instead he gave long speeches that did little to give an answer. Every question was another opportunity for a long discourse, and if I suggested that he had not actually answered my question, he argued that my question was unclear. I was getting nowhere. It seemed to me that his answers were merely spreading quite a bit of impressive dust around, and around and around. But the jury did seem impressed.

I had not expected such a performance. When David had deposed Rowley, with very similar questions only a few months before, his answers had been brief and to the point— and often helpful to our argument in the case. But this time Rowley was going on and on, and not only could I not manage to stop him, but he was winning over the jury. The jury might not have understood much of what he said, but, I was sure, they liked the somewhat bloated grandeur of the way he said it.

I left the courtroom worried. Only the day before, Gary Parsons had approached us with a settlement, and although it was substantially more than the meager figure they had offered early in the case, I believed Valerie deserved better and could do better. David and Sandy Lakey thought about the offer and then said they would be guided by my advice—*I trust you,* E.G. Sawyer had said. Then only one day later I had shown myself almost powerless against a shrewd expert defense witness, and I was worried. That evening, David, Laurie, Bill, and I sat in our offices and talked about what to do next, and for the first time in the trial our spirits were low.

"Look," I said, "there's something I've never tried before. Let's look at David's deposition of this guy and come up with three or four short answers that Rowley made back then to three or four good questions. We'll blow up those questions and put them on an easel for the jury to see, and then ask them as if for the first time. If he goes on like he did today, I'll hit him with blowups of the answers he gave before."

The next morning I began my cross-examination, "Dr. Rowley, it seemed we had some problems communicating yesterday."

"Actually, Mr. Edwards," the expert said, "I don't think we had a problem communicating. It's that your questions didn't make sense."

Jurors tittered. They liked Rowley.

I conceded the possibility that that might have been true.

And then I continued, "In fact, Dr. Rowley, it's for that reason I wrote out the questions I wanted to ask you today."

I put the first question on the easel. The expert frowned.

The question was straightforward, and it was not very important, but the engineer's answer was. For several minutes he went on and on and on, just as impressive—I guess—as he had been the day before. But this time I asked him to slow down so I could write out his answer word by word. It filled page after page of poster-size sheets, and I stacked those sheets one by one on a second easel.

"Now, Dr. Rowley," I said, "would it surprise you to learn that several months ago you were asked that same question in a deposition with Mr. Kirby? And your answer was . . ." I moved a placard that hid the bottom of the page of the deposition. There below the question I had just asked was the answer he had given months before. There were two words: "Yes, sir."

Rowley looked stern, but he agreed that indeed that had been his answer.

I asked him a second question, and again Rowley went on for a minute or two—although not as long as before, and with a little less confidence. Again I pulled away the placard that hid the answer he had given at the earlier deposition. And again two words: "Yes, sir."

Behind my back I could hear a juror laugh.

I put up a third blowup with a placard at the bottom, and I asked a third question. This one was important—and Rowley knew it. He scowled as he tried to recall his deposition reply. But this time I was bluffing. We hadn't asked him the question before.

Now he was cautious, and this time his response was very short. Two words: "No, sir."

No one laughed when he gave that response. I had a sense that the jury had come to see through him and maybe to distrust him, which was more important. Of course I did not move the placard this time, for it had nothing beneath it, and not long after that I ended my cross-examination.

I hoped the jury had lost some respect for the testimony given by the defense's expert witness, but I was still worried about having just refused a pretty substantial settlement. And so after the defense rested, I called Charles Manning, our own expert witness, back to the stand. I hoped he could offer some general rebuttal to whatever good impression Rowley had left behind.

But there was a problem: Manning was sick. He was in the bathroom, very sick. We asked for a few minutes and Judge Farmer sent the jury away. Half an hour later our engineering consultant emerged, ashen but better.

"Mr. Manning," I began, "we had to take a little break there. Are you feeling okay?"

"Sure," our expert said. "I just had to pass a kidney stone. And look—I did."

He turned to the jury box and held up the stone for their inspection.

• • •

For the two months the trial lasted, I worked every night except Christmas Eve and Christmas Day. For so many reasons I had to work. That year we didn't throw our big Christmas party, and although we did buy a tree and put some ornaments on it, we didn't set up the second tree that Wade and Cate had always decorated by themselves. In other years, Elizabeth and I would put on Christmas music and watch while Wade and Cate would pull out their own box of ornaments and set to work. Wade was older and so he felt a responsibility to balance the ornaments all over the tree, but Cate would just stand there and put on a ton of ornaments in just one spot at the bottom—while her eyes gleamed with pride. So in the end, in spite of Wade's best efforts, the splendor of the tree was sometimes a sorry lopsided affair—but it was beautiful. It was our real Christmas tree, and so it will remain. We gave each other only a few gifts the Christmas of 1996, and although we smiled over them and thanked each other very much, they did not matter, for what we really wanted we could not have. We took a Christmas wreath to Oakwood Cemetery and gave it to Wade, and the kind staff there gave us a candle, which they said would burn for days.

While my work for Valerie Lakey gave me refuge from despair, Elizabeth had nowhere to go. I have always worked hard for my clients, but it was different with the Lakey case, different for reasons I do not fully understand even now. I believe that in some way the Lakeys' loss had come together with my great loss, and so I worked and worked and worked for something bigger than that case, bigger even than that lovely little girl. In those months Elizabeth at first spent every day and every night at the learning lab, but then came the Christmas holidays when the high school was on break and the learning lab was closed. Elizabeth remained at home, and she was alone so much of the time. At night over dinner we would talk about our day—about my day, that is. Her fine analytical mind would come alive and she would help me in ways I cannot begin to number. It is hard to understand how she did it, and how we did it. In those days and nights we found places in our hearts we had not known.

. . .

I addressed the jury a final time on Friday afternoon, January 10.

"Three times during this trial," I began, "you all had a clear, perfectly clear picture, a looking-glass picture, into the heart of Sta-Rite Industries." I named them. First, when a Sta-Rite official stated in his deposition that he believed that his company had no responsibility to provide any warning of a serious hazard. Second, when the general counsel stated that, even though Sta-Rite knew a warning was necessary, it was "absolutely appropriate" to release the anti-vortex cover without such a warning. And finally, when the jury heard me read aloud the Sta-Rite's product safety coordinator's letter after he had been asked about what response he was making to the injuries caused by defective pool drain covers, when he'd said, "What is wrong with this man? Tell him to shut up. I have no intentions of answering these questions. And doesn't he know this kind of thing should never be put in writing?"

"What you have, and I really want you to form a mental picture about this," I said, "is a perfect picture of corporate indifference. Absolute corporate indifference.

"Now, I want to ask you to do something for me. I want you to take that picture and put it on one side. And right beside it, right beside it, I ask you to put this picture. On Friday exactly a month ago, at about nine o'clock in the morning, and you all were sitting right where you are now, an eight-

year-old girl walked through that door and up to the witness stand. You saw her. You watched her. She's sweet, gorgeous, frail, and very quiet. Very quiet. And she tried her best
to answer the questions that I was asking her. She didn't—
remember, she didn't want to talk about being hooked up. But
she did the best she could.

"And what you have—can you visualize it? Can you remember? I need you to remember. What you have is a perfect
picture of absolute innocence. Absolute innocence.

"Now, I want you to put those pictures side by side. Absolute corporate indifference"—I paused and made a fist with
my left hand—"and absolute innocence." And then another
fist with my right hand. "And what you have been doing for
the last seven weeks is you have been watching what happens
when absolute corporate indifference collides with absolute
innocence." I brought my fists together. "That's what this case
is. That is what this case is about. And that is why you are
here.

"And you have seen the result, haven't you?" I held up the
Sta-Rite drain cover, and I continued, "You understand now
that this piece of plastic is the only thing that stands between
the children and the hidden, deadly hazard. And you know
that most of the world has no idea that this hazard exists. You
know all these things. Sta-Rite knew all those things in 1987."

Sta-Rite had come into the courtroom and, despite what it
knew, had asked the jury to agree that it was all right for it to
have done nothing at all. And when I reminded each juror that
"if your verdict is nothing else, it is your personal, moral, and
ethical stamp of approval. Are you going to give it to them?
Are you?"

The courtroom was completely silent.

"I'm going to ask you questions, questions for you to answer without me arguing to you, for you to answer. How could it be fairer?" And so I asked. "Knowing what you now know and knowing what Sta-Rite knew in 1987, I have these questions for you: Would you put a warning on that cover? Would you? Would you put a warning on it? . . . Would you leave the cover design the way it was originally designed with these tabs that—I assume you all have figured out by now— serve no purpose at all? . . . And last, if the only thing between these children and what happened to Valerie are screws in this cover, would you do something to try to make sure the screws stay with it? Would you do that?" The jurors nodded.

"Are those exotic, unreasonable things to ask?" The jurors shook their heads.

Then my daughter Cate walked into the packed courtroom. David saw her and motioned to the front row where someone had left a space for her. I had not known she was coming. She had never heard me speak to a jury before. My family knew that the people I represented needed every bit of my attention, and so they had always left me at the courtroom door. Even Elizabeth never came to my trials. I regretted that Wade had never come. And now for the first time, for the one time I needed a child of my own there, without my asking, Cate had come.

I talked about the other culpable parties. Medfield's volunteer pool operator. He'd screwed down the big pool's drain cover because it would otherwise have floated away and because it had an embossed warning that said, "Use screws to keep cover secured to drain at all times." But because the plastic prongs did in fact seem to hold the wading pool drain cover in place—and there was no warning—he never even thought of affixing it with screws. In any event, I said, Medfield's people weren't experts like Sta-Rite's people were. They didn't know about the dangers of suction entrapment. And what's more, an accident like Valerie's had never before happened at Medfield.

"How many times has it happened to them?" I asked, gesturing to the Sta-Rite officials at the defendants' table. "When it happened to them the first time, what did they do to insure that this would never happen again? What did they do the second time? What did they do the third time, the fourth time, the fifth time, the sixth time, the seventh time, the eighth time?"

Then I approached the jury rail. I laid out a dozen Sta-Rite drain covers that had been produced since 1984. I said that although the chairman of the Product Safety Commission had exhorted pool companies to implement changes, "They haven't done a thing. I guess what they'll say in every courtroom across the country is, 'This is a problem that ought to be fixed by dual drains. There ought to be a law requiring dual drains.' I agree. The problem is that there are pools all over this country that don't have dual drains. They're everywhere. This," I said, gesturing to the drain covers, "is the only safeguard now, until the law is changed in fifty states. . . . You ask yourself: Is it not responsible and fair to ask these companies to do their part? I'm telling you, if they don't do their part, this is going to keep happening and kids are going to keep getting hurt."

I discussed the law and how Sta-Rite had essentially conceded that it had not issued a warning about the dangers of suction entrapment if its drain cover was not secured with screws. I reminded the jurors that under the doctrine of joint and several liability, Sta-Rite could be found liable even if the county and the pool club were also negligent. And finally, I said, under the law of alteration and modification, "they have to prove to you to your satisfaction that an ordinary, reasonable person would have known if those screws weren't in that cover, this accident would have happened." I stayed on the issue of alteration or modification for several minutes. Even though I felt confident about the evidence we had submitted, I did not forget those four mock trials that had been lost on this precise issue.

At last I turned to the matter of Valerie's damages. The lifetime of intravenous TPN through the central line or catheter in her chest, the countless surgeries, the continual discomfort— "She has in front of her an extraordinarily hard journey," I said. "And she needs all the help she can get. . . . Pain will be with her all the time. So what is reasonable and fair? What is reasonable and fair for all of the pain she's had, for the pain she now has, and for the next fifty, sixty years?"

Although I had talked to Elizabeth about what I would say next and I had thought about it for days, I did not know what actual words would come. I only knew what I needed to say. So much of the trial was behind me and in me that I knew that the right words would be there when I needed them. I had held them in my pocket for days, and I now just had to pull them out.

"There was a wonderful, wonderful thing written this past spring by a writer—a wonderful writer for *The News & Observer,* who was talking about a tragedy that had occurred. It wasn't this tragedy, but his words apply so beautifully to this case.

"It involved the death of a young boy who shouldn't have died, and what he wrote was this: 'We have to gather around this family, not because we understand what they're going through, but because they have to know we share their pain. Our feelings—our terrible feelings—prove that we really all are part of the same family. Their loss was our loss. Their child was our child.' "

I thought of my son. And then I continued, "The responsibility that we have to our children is the most awesome responsibility that we can have. You all now have that responsibility. It's about to go from us to you. And it is not just responsibility for Valerie; it is responsibility for all children. . . . There are thirteen children that we know about so far. Thirteen children. Valerie is unfortunately not the last. You heard about a child three months ago who died caught on an open drain, the cover not being screwed down, in New Jersey. It's happening. It's continuing to happen. It's not whether it's going to happen. It's when.

"So who's next? Whose child is next?"

I was nearing the end of my argument. "Once I sit down, once I sit down and once you all go into that jury room, there's not a thing in the world I can do for Valerie." I looked at each of them. I trusted them, as I trust all juries, and yet I hated to let Valerie go. I wanted them to care as much about protecting her as I cared.

"I want to leave you with one thought." I couldn't let go yet. "When Sandy was testifying, she told you about a conversation she had with Valerie. And what she said is, Valerie said to her, 'Mommy, I don't think anybody's ever going to want to marry me.'

"And Sandy said, 'Well, Valerie, why do you say that?'

"She said, 'Well, because of my button.'

"And Sandy said, 'Oh, that's not true.' And then she said,

'Valerie, I'm sorry, so sorry, that this happened to you. I wish it had happened to me instead.'

"You remember her answer? 'Mommy, don't say that. I never want this to happen to anybody else.'

"Only you—only you—have the power to make that wish come true."

After Judge Farmer excused the jury and called for a recess, my daughter pushed her way through the railing, and we held each other.

• • •

On the morning of January 13, 1997, the jury began deliberation. When they returned to the courtroom later that day, they had awarded David, Sandy, and Valerie Lakey $25 million as compensatory damages for Sta-Rite's negligence. Sta-Rite said that if the Lakeys would agree not to pursue punitive damages, it would agree not to appeal. They would settle the case for the amount of the verdict.

Sandy and David Lakey did not celebrate, for although their daughter's life had just changed in an important way, much remained unchanged. Valerie's colostomy bag would eventually be removed, but she would need to be hooked to intravenous feed tubes every night. She would suffer recurrent bacterial infections to her central line, requiring hospitalization, and the constant discomfort common to short bowel syndrome. There would always be the threat of liver damage, and the risk of such damage to her life itself.

In her fight to live a normal life—to enjoy that life and meet big challenges—Valerie will win. But in spite of her spirit and the great love and care of her parents, the great physical and emotional strain on her will never end. Nothing can change the fact that she faces a long struggle she should never have known, one it would have been so easy for her not to have known at all. I felt outrage at such injustice, and I continue to feel it now.

• • •

The other night when Elizabeth and I were talking to a friend about what would be in this book, I told him there was one thing I surely couldn't say. It would sound too arrogant, too insolent by a mile. But I will tell it anyway. I told him that when I worked for the Lakeys, I was the best lawyer of my life, and I did the best lawyering of my life. I knew that there was no one who could have beaten me in that courtroom. Yet knowing that gave me no pride or pleasure, for at that time it was my minimum requirement for myself, the very least I demanded of myself, and other than that it was next to nothing. In those months as I struggled to come alive again, more than life itself I needed to do something strong and good, and I would give it to Valerie—and also in my own private way to my son. I wanted to offer them tribute, and it would be worthy. And yes, I worked. I knew every detail and every fact of Valerie's case, and I had thought out every move and every step and every half step, and I knew every law, and every mistake I had ever made or could ever make. I watched the jury as I had never watched a jury before, and I knew them—I knew every one of them. I can't imagine what they saw when they looked back at me.

Strange as it is for me to say it, I was lucky. When I stood before that jury, I knew I could keep my secret and hold it tight. When I spoke of the injustice that had come to Valerie, I was also silently protesting the absolute injustice of my son's brief life—but no one knew what I was saying. Each day I was allowed to describe my pain, the ache of unbearable pain, and I spoke instead about the Lakeys' and I would look over at them. I would speak about Valerie's struggles day after day and those she would face in the years ahead, but a voice inside me was speaking too of the lovely years my son had lost, even the hours he had lost, and I was putting him to bed at night when he was still a child. And I spoke of my wife Elizabeth's pain—but I would say Sandy Lakey's name, and the jury would turn their heads and look at her.

In the late fall of 1996, I had the great privilege to be Valerie's voice when she needed me. And the great fortune to be her voice when I needed her.

AFTERWORD

I HAVE SPOKEN OF DECENCY quite often in this book, and I am happy that I have. As I have said, when I grew up in Robbins, I had no idea that there was any other kind of world out there—any world that knew less hard work or more bright things or more things of any sort. But I hope I have made it clear that I feel lucky to have grown up in a world where so many people knew what was really important in life. And it was the greatest gift to have a son who knew just as surely what was important and what must remain important. One evening when I was troubling over what to put into this final chapter, Elizabeth showed me the letter Alyse Tharpe had written to Wade, a letter inspired by Wade. Of course I remembered the day we first received it, but when I read it again that night, I read it as if for the first time. When she wrote that letter, Alyse already knew what mattered, and usually that takes many years—if we get there at all. It would be a fine thing for anyone to feel in any lifetime that he or she had managed to express the absolutely sure decency that my son knew, that Alyse expressed in every sentence and every word of her letter.

Nothing I have done has gotten close to that yet, and I suspect nothing will. But I hope to continue to try.

When I began to think about this book, I did not know how much I would say about Wade, or particularly about his death, and I thought it would be best not to say that much about it. But as I attempted to explain my life as an advocate and as a man, I found it impossible not to speak of him. As much as anyone is—as much as my other children, Cate, Emma Claire, and Jack, as much as my parents, my grandmother, and my wife—Wade is who I am. As I have progressed through this strange task of putting together a book, I have found—just as people said and I never believed—that a book has a life of its own. Although at the start this task was hard even to begin, as Elizabeth and I thought about what would go into this last chapter, so many things came into our heads—everything at once, it seemed. Now our study is piled up with letters, diaries, transcripts, notes, memos, and many old pictures. As I look around the room, I see that almost every scrap of paper touches on the life of my family and on the life of my son—and I discover that it is his life, not his death, that has inspired me. That was true every day Wade was living, and it has been true every day since his death.

It may be an indulgence to again quote a few words of my son's, but I think it is an indulgence that you will permit me. Wade completed a Colorado Outward Bound mountain-climbing program when he was only fifteen, just before we climbed Mount Kilimanjaro. The Outward Bound program asks its participants to write a journal of their experiences. After Wade died, I read his journal, which he never expected to be read by me or by anyone, and then I read portions of the journal at his funeral. Everything that I value is in his words.

> I have learned a lot of things so far. I have learned not to take anything I have at home for granted. That especially goes for my family. I am going to try to not fight with my family. I now realize all they do for me, and I think I need to do more for them. I have also learned, mostly from the [mountain] pass, that even though something may seem impossible, if I put my best effort into it, it can be conquered. I feel that I can apply that to my life and obstacles I face on the way. I have also learned that I have a great life, and I need to be thankful for what I have. I have great friends and family. This trip, I think, will have a pretty big impact on my life. I am starting to be glad that I am here. . . .
>
> Although I am glad that I have been doing this, there isn't a moment that I don't wish to be home. That is mostly because I miss my family so much. This is the longest that I have ever been away from them without any contact. I always think about the 29th when I get to see them again. I have made it the whole time without crying, until now. . . .
>
> Rock climbing is probably one of the scariest and most thrilling things that I have ever done. I made it all the way to the top. I didn't get a chance to try the really hard one because I was helping another group member for a long time. I think that rock climbing was an amazing experience and I am really glad that I got to try it, and even conquer it. It was so satisfying to slap the top

of the rope but then so scary to get back to the ground. As we were walking back to camp today, I just kept thinking about Cate. I haven't seen her in so long, and I really miss her. Even though we fight a lot, I love her with all my heart. I can't wait till this course is over. But don't get me wrong, I am very glad that I am getting this great experience. . . .

The course director said that the solo is where you become a man. I disagree with that. I think that you become a man by slowly maturing. I think that it takes different experiences to help you mature and I think that you never really stop maturing and growing as a person. This solo, and this course for that matter, are helping me realize that I can make it alone. I think that I will be okay when it is time for me to enter the real world. I think that my parents have done, and continue to do, an outstanding job raising me.

I think that if I just put my mind to it, I can accomplish all my goals. So far my toughest challenge on the course was the first day. It was not only tough physically but also mentally. When I first looked at it, I thought that there was no way I could do it. That made all of it harder. Halfway through it, I looked up and thought that I had already spent everything I had. That made it all that much sweeter to finally make it to the top. I know that when this course is over I will be very proud of myself and very self confident. Whenever I have an obstacle to overcome in the future, I will think back to this course and know that I can conquer it. More than any other goal that I have set for myself I want to show my love and appreciation to my family for all that they have done for me. There is only one other member in my group whose parents are not separated. That just makes me realize that I have yet another thing in my life to be thankful for. I know that I don't deserve all that I get but I hope that I will someday be able to say that I deserve it. I really want to do something great with my life. I want to start a family when I grow up. I am going to be as good a parent to my kids as my parents are to me. But more than anything, when I die, I want to be able to say that I had a great life. So far I have had a wonderful life (and I hope it keeps up).

It's just after Easter 2003, and I am working to finish this book. Elizabeth is cooking dinner and our two young children are coloring Easter eggs—although it would be slightly more accurate to say that I am actually coloring eggs with Emma Claire, who is now five, while Jack, who has just turned three, is happily cracking boiled eggs into cups of dye. The countertop is covered with ribbons of watery primary colors. Jack slips below the counter, which sends Emma Claire into a deep belly laugh. Cate, who has stayed at Princeton to finish her junior paper, calls in the middle of chaos. She misses us. She wishes she could be here with us.

I hang up the phone as Jack knocks over his cup of red dye and Emma Claire again doubles over in laughter. Jack laughs because Emma Claire is laughing—with no idea that she is laughing at him—and Elizabeth lunges for the paper towels. This is my family and we are happy. And Wade—who sat at that same kitchen counter when he read us the first paragraph of his first short story—is part of that happiness every day.

As Wade knew, there's a lot to be learned in this world.

During my years in the United States Senate, I have learned a great deal about policies and programs, about procedures and politics, but I know that what was most important was learned somewhere else and often many years before. As I have worked to serve the people of my state and my country, I have come to understand that there could have been no better experience than that of having swept the floors in that mill, or seeing my father taking notes in front of the education classes on television, or watching my parents at the kitchen table as they tried to find a way to send me to college. And there could have been no substitute for the fear and joy I felt at the birth of each of our four children, for the way the world changed when my son died, or for the chance I had to work—for twenty fine years—beside remarkable men and women as they fought for justice and a better life for those they loved.

The happiness I experience today is a lifetime away from the happiness I felt when I started on this path. What I learned in the intervening years was that all things were possible—all things good and all things bad. Through the fifty years I have lived and through these four cases, and dozens and dozens more, I have learned two great lessons—that there will always be heartache and struggle, and that people of strong will can make a difference. One is a sad lesson; the other is inspiring. I choose to be inspired.

ABOUT THE AUTHOR

After graduating from North Carolina State University in 1974, JOHN EDWARDS continued his education at the University of North Carolina at Chapel Hill, where he earned a law degree with honors. For the next twenty years, John dedicated his career to representing families and children hurt by the negligence of others. In 1998, John took his commitment into politics to give a voice in the United States Senate to the people he had represented throughout his career. Sworn into office on January 6, 1999, Senator John Edwards has emerged as a champion for issues affecting the daily lives of regular people in North Carolina and the nation. In North Carolina, John resides with his wife and children.

JOHN AUCHARD is a professor of English at the University of Maryland. He most recently edited *The Portable Henry James* (Penguin Putnam, 2003). He is also a travel writer who regularly writes for *The Washington Post* on destinations in the developing world. He lives in Washington, D.C.

Printed in the United States
By Bookmasters